Authenticity

Life Together Resources

Building Character Together series

Authenticity: Living a Spiritually Healthy Life

Friendship: Living a Connected Life

Faith: Living a Transformed Life

Service: Living a Meaningful Life

Influence: Living a Contagious Life

Obedience: Living a Yielded Life

Doing Life Together series

Beginning Life Together

Connecting with God's Family

Growing to Be Like Christ

Developing Your SHAPE to Serve Others

Sharing Your Life Mission Every Day

Surrendering Your Life to God's Pleasure

Experiencing Christ Together series

Beginning in Christ Together

Connecting in Christ Together

Growing in Christ Together

Serving Like Christ Together

Sharing Christ Together

Surrendering to Christ Together

building
CHARACTER
together

AUTHENTICITY

living a
Spiritually
Healthy
life

BRETT and DEE EASTMAN
TODD and DENISE WENDORFF

ZONDERVAN®

ZONDERVAN.com/
AUTHORTRACKER
follow your favorite authors

We want to hear from you. Please send your comments about this book to us in care of zreview@zondervan.com. Thank you.

ZONDERVAN®

Authenticity
Copyright © 2007 by Brett and Deanna Eastman, Todd and Denise Wendorff

Requests for information should be addressed to:

Zondervan, *Grand Rapids, Michigan 49530*

ISBN-10: 0-310-24990-2
ISBN-13: 978-0-310-24990-0

Interior design by Melissa Elenbaas

Printed in the United States of America

07 08 09 10 11 12 13 • 10 9 8 7 6 5 4 3 2 1

Contents

ACKNOWLEDGMENTS

It's been quite a ride ever since our first series was published back in 2002. Literally thousands of churches and small groups have studied the LIFE TOGETHER series to the tune of over two million copies sold. As we said back in our first series, "By the grace of God and a clear call on the hearts of a few, our dream has become a reality." Now, our dream has entered the realm of being beyond all that we could ask or imagine.

To see thousands and thousands of people step out to gather a few friends and do a Bible study with an easy-to-use DVD curriculum has been amazing. People have grown in their faith, introduced their friends to Christ, and found deeper connection with God. Thanks to God for planting this idea in our hearts. Thanks to all of those who took a risk by stepping out to lead a group for six weeks for the very first time. This has been truly amazing.

Once again, a great team was instrumental to creating this new series in community. From the start back at Saddleback with Todd and Denise Wendorff and Brett and Dee Eastman, the writing team has grown. Special thanks to John Fischer, yes, THE John Fischer, for writing all of the introductions to these studies. Also, thanks to our LIFE TOGETHER writing team: Pam Marotta, Peggy Matthews Rose, and Teri Haymaker. Last, but not least, thanks to Allen White for keeping this project on track and getting the ball in the net.

Thank you to our church families who have loved and supported us and helped us grow over the years. There are so many pastors, staff, and members that have taught us so much. We love you all.

Finally, thank you to our beloved families who have lived with us, laughed at us, and loved us through it all. We love doing our lives together with you.

OUTLINE OF
EACH SESSION

Most people want to live a healthy, balanced spiritual life, but few achieve this by themselves. And most small groups struggle to balance all of God's purposes in their meetings. Groups tend to overemphasize one of the five purposes, perhaps fellowship or discipleship. Rarely is there a healthy balance that includes evangelism, ministry, and worship. That's why we've included all of these elements in this study so you can live a healthy, balanced spiritual life over time.

A typical group session will include the following:

CONNECTING WITH GOD'S FAMILY (FELLOWSHIP). The foundation for spiritual growth is an intimate connection with God and his family. A few people who really know you and who earn your trust provide a place to experience the life Jesus invites you to live. This section of each session typically offers you two options: You can get to know your whole group by using the icebreaker question, or you can check in with one or two group members—your spiritual partner(s)—for a deeper connection and encouragement in your spiritual journey.

GROWING TO BE LIKE CHRIST (DISCIPLESHIP). Here is where you come face-to-face with Scripture. In core passages you'll explore what the Bible teaches about character through the lives of God's people in Scripture. The focus won't be on accumulating information but on how we should live in light of the Word of God. We want to help you apply the Scriptures practically, creatively, and from your heart as well as your head. At the end of the day, allowing the timeless truths from God's Word to transform our lives in Christ is our greatest aim.

FOR DEEPER STUDY. If you want to dig deeper into more Bible passages about the topic at hand, we've provided additional passages and questions. Your group may choose to do study homework ahead of each meeting in order to cover more biblical material. Or you as an individual may choose to study the For Deeper Study passages on your own. If you prefer not to do study homework, the Growing section will

9

provide you with plenty to discuss within the group. These options allow individuals or the whole group to go deeper in their study, while still accommodating those who can't do homework.

You can record your discoveries in your journal. We encourage you to read some of your insights to a friend (spiritual partner) for accountability and support. Spiritual partners may check in each week over the phone, through email, or at the beginning of the group meeting.

 DEVELOPING YOUR GIFTS TO SERVE OTHERS (MINISTRY). Jesus trained his disciples to discover and develop their gifts to serve others. God has designed you uniquely to serve him in a way no other person can. This section will help you discover and use your God-given design. It will also encourage your group to discover your unique design as a community. In this study, you'll put into practice what you've learned in the Bible study by taking a step to serve others. These simple steps will take your group on a faith journey that could change your lives forever.

 SHARING YOUR LIFE MISSION EVERY DAY (EVANGELISM). Many people skip over this aspect of the Christian life because it's scary, relationally awkward, or simply too much work for their busy schedules. But Jesus wanted all of his disciples to help outsiders connect with him, to know him personally. This doesn't mean preaching on street corners. It could mean welcoming a few newcomers into your group, hosting a short-term group in your home, or walking through this study with a friend. In this study, you'll have an opportunity to go beyond Bible study to biblical living.

 SURRENDERING YOUR LIFE FOR GOD'S PLEASURE (WORSHIP). God is most pleased by a heart that is fully his. Each group session will give you a chance to surrender your heart to God in prayer and worship. You may read a psalm together, share a page in your journal, or sing a song to close your meeting. (A LIFE TOGETHER Worship DVD/CD series, produced by Maranatha!, is available through www.lifetogether. com.) If you have never prayed aloud in a group before, no one will put pressure on you. Instead, you'll experience the support of others who are praying for you. This time will knit your hearts in community and help you surrender your hurts and dreams into the hands of the One who knows you best.

STUDY NOTES. This section provides background notes on the Bible passage(s) you examine in the Growing section. You may want to refer to these notes during your group meeting or as a reference for those doing additional study.

REFLECTIONS. Each week on the Reflections pages we provide Scriptures to read and reflect on between group meetings. We suggest you use this section to seek God at home throughout the week. This time at home should begin and end with prayer. Don't get in a hurry; take enough time to hear God's direction.

SUBGROUPS FOR DISCUSSION AND PRAYER. In some of the sessions of this series we have suggested you separate into groups of two to four for discussion or prayer. This is to assure greater participation and deeper discussion.

JOSEPH AND HIS BROTHERS

I would venture to guess that every family has at least one ornery character in it—someone who can be cantankerous, opinionated, and closed-minded to anything but the way they see the world. These people try our patience and force us to find out what love really is.

We have a person like that in our family, and I have marveled at how my wife is able to deal with him. This is what I've observed: She treats him as being important. She tells him she loves him often. She chats with him even if he doesn't have anything to say. She goes to him for advice on what he is good at.

I can't guarantee this will always happen, but what has emerged in our case is a different person than we thought. Someone with a softer center. He's still quite rough around the edges, but something has shown up I would call loyalty, to the extent that when other more accepting members of the family are not available or don't care, he is the one who comes through every time. My kids call him Grandpa Grouch, but they use the term endearingly, because they've come to see something else.

What they see is what my wife saw and brought out by her patient attention. Paul says that love "believes all things" (1 Corinthians 13:7 NASB), and I think that when you faithfully believe something about someone, and treat them as if they have what you believe in, you create an environment for that very thing to grow—it can even be an interest in the things of God.

CONNECTING WITH GOD'S FAMILY   20 MIN.

Few things demand more character than difficult family relationships. And because we are all flawed people, it's rarely the case that someone gets along famously with every member of their extended family.

1. Take time in your group to introduce yourselves to each other. Then a few of you answer the following questions: Who do you have the hardest time getting along with in your family and why? How do you naturally respond to them? What would be a godly response?

2. Whether your group is just forming or has been together for a while, it's good to review and consider your shared values from time to time. You'll find a Small Group Agreement on pages 97–98 containing those values we have found over the years to be the most useful in building and sustaining healthy, balanced groups. It's a good idea to pick one or two values to focus on to guide you through this study and help you build deeper relationships. If your group is new, you may find the Frequently Asked Questions on pages 94–96 helpful.

   After assessing your group values you might want to go to the Small Group Calendar on page 99 to map out your meeting schedule and holidays so everyone can plan ahead for this study.

3. While you are working through the rest of this session, pass around a sheet of paper or one of you pass your study guide opened to the Small Group Roster on pages 124–125. Have everyone write down their contact information. Ask someone to make copies or type up a list with everyone's information and email it to the group this week.

GROWING TO BE LIKE CHRIST   40 MIN.

The story of Joseph and his brothers is a colorful one full of rivalry, treachery, forgiveness, and salvation; it shows how God is at work, not in spite of our foibles and our sins, but directly through them, to bring about his plan for us and for others. "You intended to harm me," Joseph told his brothers at story's end, "but God intended it for good" (Genesis 50:20).

Throughout this incredible story, something happened in the lives of its players that happens just as importantly to us: God uses the people in our lives to shape who we are, and are to become, and it will be our humble submission to this process that will produce character in us.

But this character cannot be created in isolation. Though it is important to have time alone with God, we don't mature only in this way. Maturity of character happens as we rub against (and in some cases bounce off) one another. Character comes out of living in community with others.

In Joseph's case, it was his brothers who forced him into situations that would seem to stretch anyone to a breaking point. Jealous over the special treatment Joseph received from their father, and further incensed by his interpretation of dreams that put him in a position to rule over them, his brothers plotted to kill Joseph while they were away from home grazing their flocks. One of the older brothers, feeling somewhat responsible, decided they should sell him instead to a traveling caravan headed for Egypt. "After all, he is our brother, our own flesh and blood" (Genesis 37:27). Tearing Joseph's robe and splattering it with blood from a slaughtered animal, they returned to their father, Jacob, with the bad news. Joseph must have been attacked and killed by a ferocious animal; all they could find of him was his torn, bloody coat.

Meanwhile, Joseph is sold to Potiphar, the captain of Pharaoh's guard, where his responsibility and reliability earn him a position as manager of all Potiphar's affairs. Even after he is falsely accused of trying to take advantage of Potiphar's wife and is thrown into jail, he ends up managing the jail. When Pharaoh is troubled by dreams none of his diviners can interpret, Joseph is summoned from jail to interpret them. The dreams turn out to be about seven years of plenty followed by seven years of famine that Egypt is about to endure. Joseph's advice: store up grain the first seven years to sustain the nation through the famine. The king is so impressed with Joseph that he puts him in charge of the whole project, and then of his whole kingdom. Thus it happens, when Joseph's brothers journey to Egypt during the famine years, they have to come and humble themselves before Joseph with their request for food, thus fulfilling his childhood predictions.

Joseph immediately recognizes them as his brothers, but they do not recognize him. Joseph decides to maintain his cover and proceeds to put his brothers' loyalty to the test. He finds out he has a younger brother and that his father, Jacob, is still alive. A few times during this charade, Joseph is so overcome with emotion he has to leave the room in order to compose himself. Finally, no longer able to conceal his identity from them, he reveals himself to the wonder and disbelief of his brothers.

Read Genesis 45:1–7:

> *Then Joseph could no longer control himself before all his attendants, and he cried out, "Have everyone leave my presence!" So there was no one with Joseph when he made himself known to his brothers. ²And he wept so loudly that the Egyptians heard him, and Pharaoh's household heard about it. ³Joseph said to his brothers, "I am Joseph! Is my father still living?" But his brothers were not able to answer him, because they were terrified at his presence.*
>
> *⁴Then Joseph said to his brothers, "Come close to me." When they had done so, he said, "I am your brother Joseph, the one you sold into Egypt! ⁵And now, do not be distressed and do not be angry with yourselves for selling me here, because it was to save lives that God sent me ahead of you. ⁶For two years now there has been famine in the land, and for the next five years there will not be plowing and reaping. ⁷But God sent me ahead of you to preserve for you a remnant on earth and to save your lives by a great deliverance."*

4. Joseph did not immediately tell his brothers who he was. Why do you suppose Joseph took so long to reveal himself to them? When he did reveal himself, what was his attitude (verse 5)?

5. How did Joseph feel toward his brothers? How do you suppose he kept himself from bitterness and anger? After all, they tried to kill him; he could have returned the favor.

6. What character qualities is Joseph exhibiting here?

Later, after Jacob dies, the brothers fear that Joseph's civility toward them was only out of respect for their father, and with Jacob dead, he will now take revenge upon them for what they did to him — with the strength of the entire Egyptian army at his disposal.

Read Genesis 50:15–21:

When Joseph's brothers saw that their father was dead, they said, "What if Joseph holds a grudge against us and pays us back for all the wrongs we did to him?" ¹⁶So they sent word to Joseph, saying, "Your father left these instructions before he died: ¹⁷'This is what you are to say to Joseph: I ask you to forgive your brothers the sins and the wrongs they committed in treating you so badly.' Now please forgive the sins of the servants of the God of your father." When their message came to him, Joseph wept.

¹⁸His brothers then came and threw themselves down before him. "We are your slaves," they said. ¹⁹But Joseph said to them, "Don't be afraid. Am I in the place of God? ²⁰You intended to harm me, but God intended it for good to accomplish what is now being done, the saving of many lives. ²¹So then, don't be afraid. I will provide for you and your children." And he reassured them and spoke kindly to them.

7. It appears that Joseph had already forgiven his brothers. When did he do that?

8. Why do you think Joseph wept? How did his brothers respond to his weeping? What was Joseph's response?

9. Can anyone in the group tell a personal story about how God turned something someone meant for evil against them into something good?

FOR DEEPER STUDY

Read Genesis 41:1–14. "When two full years had passed" is truly a significant statement. It tells us that Joseph spent at least two years, possibly more, in what was not the best of situations. Indeed, he had to shave and change his clothes just to be presentable to the king. He calls his quarters a dungeon instead of a jail. Can you even imagine what must have been going through Joseph's mind during his time in such a state?

What would he have been tempted to think?

Based on his consistent behavior before and after his imprisonment, what do you think he was doing all that time in prison?

What were the "shortcomings" of the cupbearer (Genesis 41:9; see also 40:14)? *When people are kind to us, we need to remember to return the favor.*

Joseph once defended his innocence: "For I was forcibly carried off from the land of the Hebrews, and even here I have done nothing to deserve being put in a dungeon" (Genesis 40:15). How does he handle this injustice?

Joseph has been considered a "type" of Christ. (Typological symbolism, or types, is a form of biblical interpretation that assumes that God placed anticipations of Christ in the writings of the Old Testament.) Joseph's "death" resulted in the salvation of many and when he was falsely accused and imprisoned for a crime he did not commit, he accepted his fate and served out his sentence. What other characteristics of Jesus do you see Joseph exemplifying?

DEVELOPING YOUR GIFTS TO SERVE OTHERS   15 MIN.

Joseph knew that God had been with him preparing him for what he needed to do to save both the Egyptians and his own family from starvation during the famine.

10. One habit that helps to overcome struggles while striving to reach spiritual goals is having a "spiritual partner." Pair up with someone in your group. (We suggest that men partner with men and women with women.) This person will be your spiritual partner during this study. He or she doesn't have to be your best friend but will simply encourage you to complete any goals you set for yourself during the course of this study. Following through on a resolution is tough when you're on your own, but we've found it makes all the difference to have a partner cheering us on.

On pages 100–101 is a Personal Health Plan, a chart for keeping track of your spiritual progress. Ask your leader for an additional Health Plan if you have more than one partner. In the box that says "WHO are you connecting with spiritually?" write your partner's name. You can see that the health plan contains space for you to record the ups and downs of your progress each week in the column labeled "My Progress." And now with your spiritual partner you don't have to do it alone, but together with a friend.

When you check in with your partner each week, the "Partner's Progress" column on this chart will provide a place to record your partner's progress throughout this study. To help you use your Personal Health Plan, you'll find a Sample Personal Health Plan filled in as an example on page 103.

For now, don't worry about the WHAT, WHERE, WHEN, and HOW questions on your Health Plan.

11. How can this group help you discover what God is preparing you for? Rotating hosts and leaders is a great way to begin to discover what your gifts are, and it is one of the values we highly recommend for your group.

   Whether you have led a group before or not, your group will give you all the encouragement you need before, during, and after the session. Some groups like to let the host lead the meeting each week; others like to let one person host while another person leads.

   The Small Group Calendar on page 99 is a tool for planning who will host and lead each meeting and who will provide refreshments. Take a few minutes to plan for your next five meetings. Don't pass this up! It will greatly impact your group.

SHARING YOUR LIFE MISSION EVERY DAY   5 MIN.

   Joseph embraced the opportunities and circumstances God placed before him and, through God's power, let his character be molded into a vessel of God's will. As a result, he was a powerful witness for God.

12. When have you experienced God providing an opportunity for your life to be a testimony of Christ to someone who needs to know him? How can you be sure your example reveals Christ?

SURRENDERING YOUR LIFE FOR GOD'S PLEASURE   15–20 MIN.

   Not only did Joseph trust God in every circumstance in his life, but he gave him all the credit for every good thing that came from them—he could see God's hand at work in his life.

13. Share your prayer requests and take a few minutes to pray together as a group. Each person pray one- or two-sentence

prayers. Pray that you would be willing, open, and responsive to God's leading in your life. Be sure to write your prayer requests on the Prayer and Praise Report on page 22.

14. A crucial part of growing spiritually is communicating with God. Developing our communication with God involves prayer, reading his Word, and reflecting on what he is telling us through his Word. If you engage in these activities over the next six weeks, you will see growth in your ability to discern God's will for you. We have provided a Reflections section at the end of each session. For this session you will find the Reflections beginning on page 23. Each of these includes five days of Scripture for you to read and reflect upon. There is also a place for you to record your thoughts. On day six, reflect on what you have looked at in this session and during your Reflections time this week. This important habit will help you grow closer to God throughout this study.

STUDY NOTES

The one you sold into Egypt! Joseph is recalling the incident recorded in Genesis 37:12 – 36, when out of jealousy his brothers faked his death by selling him to the Midianites, who in turn sold him to Potiphar in Egypt.

Famine. Joseph predicted this seven-year famine when interpreting Pharaoh's dreams (Genesis 41). "A text from Siheil in southern Egypt dating from the second century BC tells of a seven-year famine followed by years of plenty in the time of Djoser (c. 2600 BC)." (Gordon Wenham, *Genesis 16 – 50*, Word Biblical Commentary, Dallas: Word, 1994, 393.)

Preserve for you a remnant on earth. At this point, the "nation" of Israel consisted of Joseph's family. Joseph's father, Jacob, received the name Israel after his wrestling match with the angel of the Lord (Genesis 32:28). By saving his family members from famine, Joseph is preserving the promise of God to bring a savior to the earth (Genesis 3:15) as well as the promise that all nations would be blessed through his grandfather, Abraham (Genesis 15).

PRAYER AND PRAISE REPORT

Briefly share your prayer requests with the large group, making notations below. Then gather in small groups of two to four to pray for each other.

Date: _____

PRAYER REQUESTS

_____

_____

_____

_____

_____

_____

_____

_____

_____

_____

_____

_____

PRAISE REPORT

_____

_____

_____

_____

_____

_____

_____

_____

REFLECTIONS

Each day read the daily verse(s) and give prayerful consideration to what you learn about God, his Spirit, and his place in your life. Then record your thoughts, insights, or prayer in the Reflect section. On day six record a summary of what you have learned over the entire week through this study.

DAY 1   *"And we know that in all things God works for the good of those who love him, who have been called according to his purpose." (Romans 8:28)*

REFLECT: _____

_____

_____

_____

_____

_____

_____

DAY 2   *"Your attitude should be the same as that of Christ Jesus." (Philippians 2:5)*

REFLECT: _____

_____

_____

_____

_____

_____

_____

DAY 3 *"Get rid of all bitterness, rage and anger, brawling and slander, along with every form of malice." (Ephesians 4:31)*

REFLECT: _____

_____

_____

_____

_____

_____

_____

_____

_____

_____

_____

DAY 4 *"Trust in the LORD and do good; dwell in the land and enjoy safe pasture." (Psalm 37:3)*

REFLECT: _____

_____

_____

_____

_____

_____

_____

_____

_____

_____

_____

_____

DAY 5   *"Let us hold unswervingly to the hope we profess, for he who promised is faithful." (Hebrews 10:23)*

REFLECT: _____

_____

_____

_____

_____

_____

_____

_____

_____

_____

_____

_____

DAY 6   Use the following space to write any thoughts God has put in your heart and mind about the things discussed during session one and/or your Reflections time this week.

SUMMARY: _____

_____

_____

_____

_____

_____

_____

_____

_____

_____

_____

_____

FRIENDS OF A PARALYTIC

A number of years ago I encountered what can only be called an anomaly. It was a mission organization/publishing company whose staff and workers lived communally. No, this wasn't a hippie commune from the '60s. It was a community of multiple families who pooled all their resources in order to save money for the missions they enable all over the world.

It started in the 1940s when two families felt called to the mission field and decided to raise their own support. In order to cut down on expenses, they lived together in one large house. Soon they discovered they were making good money and decided what God really wanted them to do is finance others to the mission field with their financial successes and the money they were saving by communal living. Soon more families joined them and for a while they manufactured recreation vehicles, and later sold that business and began a Christian publishing house. All the while their community was expanding. Under this unique system, they have been able to supply 100 percent of the financial requirements of a number of missionaries across the globe.

To visit this community now is to discover a normal group of people living in a much different manner than most of us. If you need a ladder, you go check one out from the equipment building. If you need a car, you go check one out from the garage. If you're hungry, you eat in the cafeteria. And all this sharing puts them in close contact with each other. To some this may seem stifling, but it is only relative to what we have come to call our "independence." Independence sometimes translates to aloneness.

Not that everyone should adopt this model, but just knowing someone can do this gives you a different perspective on things. It makes you realize that what we call normal isn't necessarily right. Our society creates a big shell for us to live in apart from one another. If we are to grow in character like Christ we are going to need to figure out ways of coming out from under our shells and being more dependent on each other. This group is a good start.

CONNECTING WITH GOD'S FAMILY   20 MIN.

We live in a society in which everyone is expected to be self-sufficient. We all have our own homes, our own cars, our own insurance, and our own problems. Compared to other world cultures and even our own not-so-distant history of extended families, we live relatively isolated lives. Someone said it takes a village to survive. The problem is: we don't have any villages anymore. We live alone, suffer alone, and die alone. There is a deep, unexpressed need in the twenty-first century for community.

Participating in this study group was most likely not a step easily taken. You can all congratulate yourself for getting this far.

1. Welcome any newcomers to your group. Introduce yourselves and tell how you came to be a part of this group. What does it mean to be a part of a community? What do you like or not like about it?

2. Sit with your spiritual partner. Turn to the Personal Health Assessment on pages 104 – 105 and take a few minutes right now to rate yourself in each area. You won't have to share your scores with the group. Discuss the following with your spiritual partner:

   • What's one area that is going well and one area that's not going as well? Don't be embarrassed; everybody struggles in one area or another.

   • Take a moment and write in a simple step (or goal) under "WHAT is your next step for growth?" on the Personal Health Plan on page 100.

   Share your goal with your spiritual partner and plan to give updates on your progress throughout this study.

GROWING TO BE LIKE CHRIST   40 MIN.

When Jesus taught, people gathered! People who "needed" healing, love, forgiveness, wisdom, or who wanted those things for someone close to them.

For the paralytic, it was healing. It is unknown what type of paralysis the paralytic had, but it is known from Scripture that it prevented him from walking. He was completely dependent on others.

If not for his friends, the paralytic would not have been able to see Jesus that day. But if not for his need of Jesus, he would not have been healed.

For most of us, our physical needs don't compare with those of the paralytic in this story, but we all need Jesus. And for most of us, someone introduced us.

Read Luke 5:17–26:

> One day as he was teaching, Pharisees and teachers of the law, who had come from every village of Galilee and from Judea and Jerusalem, were sitting there. And the power of the Lord was present for him to heal the sick. [18]Some men came carrying a paralytic on a mat and tried to take him into the house to lay him before Jesus. [19]When they could not find a way to do this because of the crowd, they went up on the roof and lowered him on his mat through the tiles into the middle of the crowd, right in front of Jesus. [20]When Jesus saw their faith, he said, "Friend, your sins are forgiven."
>
> [21]The Pharisees and the teachers of the law began thinking to themselves, "Who is this fellow who speaks blasphemy? Who can forgive sins but God alone?"
>
> [22]Jesus knew what they were thinking and asked, "Why are you thinking these things in your hearts? [23]Which is easier: to say, 'Your sins are forgiven,' or to say, 'Get up and walk'? [24]But that you may know that the Son of Man has authority on earth to forgive sins . . ." He said to the paralyzed man, "I tell you, get up, take your mat and go home." [25]Immediately he stood up in front of them, took what he had been lying on and went home praising God. [26]Everyone was amazed and gave praise to God. They were filled with awe and said, "We have seen remarkable things today."

3. What can you assume from this story about the relationship between the paralytic and his friends?

4. What character qualities do his friends embody?

5. What would these friends have had to overcome in order to bring the paralytic to Jesus?

6. Say you're the owner of this house. How would you deal with this? What would your reaction say about what you value?

7. Do you have someone in your life who you would go to any length to help? Do you have anyone who would do this for you? Share some stories about being on either side of this.

8. Whose faith made this man whole? Pick someone whom your entire group can be responsible for bringing before the Lord. Let it be more than just a prayer; ask God to show you something tangible you together can do for this person.

FOR DEEPER STUDY

Why did Jesus forgive the sins of the paralytic before healing him? Which is more important, having your sins forgiven or getting healed?

Read Galatians 6:2–5. How does this relate to the story of the paralytic? What is the difference between carrying someone else's burden (verse 2) and carrying one's own load (verse 5)? Come up with some examples of a load we each are expected to carry and a burden that we need help with.

DEVELOPING YOUR GIFTS TO SERVE OTHERS 10 MIN.

The friends of the paralytic were committed to meeting the needs of their friend. Time spent with friends develops our ability to see one another's needs.

9. Take time now to begin planning a group social event to be held at the end of this study. Pick a date between the end of this study and the start of the next. You can do this in many creative ways. A few include:

- Share a meal together prior to your group time. Ask someone to coordinate the date, time and place. Make sure the information gets out to everyone.

- Go out to dinner together or have a potluck at someone's home.

- Plan a women's night out while the guys take care of the kids; then plan another evening for the guys to go out while the women watch the kids. If no one in your group has children, designate a night for the women to have a "girls' night out" and the men to have a "guys' night out."

Get out your calendars and schedule a date. Remember, fellowship is all about living life together.

10. Is anyone missing from your group this week? If anyone is absent, someone volunteer to call or email them and let them know they were missed. It's very important for people to know they are cared about.

SHARING YOUR LIFE MISSION EVERY DAY   10 MIN.

The friends of the paralytic realized that Jesus could meet their friend's need. They didn't let obstacles keep them from bringing him to Jesus.

11. We've found that groups that focus on reaching out to unbelievers grow much deeper in their relationships than those that look only inward. Who are the people in your life who need to meet Jesus or know him more deeply? The Circles of Life diagram below will help you think of the various people you come in contact with on a regular basis. Prayerfully write down two or three names in each of the circles.

The beginning of a new study is a wonderful time to welcome a few friends into your group. Which of the people in your circles could you invite? How can you help your friends overcome obstacles to joining your group? Does your friend need a ride to the group? Help with child care? What can you, or your group, do to help?

CIRCLES OF LIFE

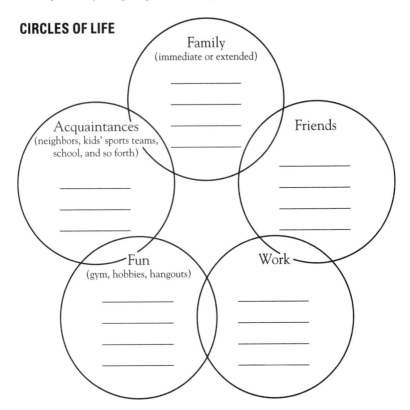

12. Is there someone who you wouldn't invite to your group but still needs a connection? Would you be willing to have lunch or coffee with that person, catch up on life, and share something you've learned from this study?

SURRENDERING YOUR LIFE FOR GOD'S PLEASURE   15–20 MIN.

Luke 5:26 tells us that all the people who saw Jesus heal the paralytic were amazed and praised God. They had seen remarkable things that day.

13. Share your prayer requests and record them on the Prayer and Praise Report provided on page 35. Have any previous prayer requests been answered? If so, celebrate these answers to prayer. Then, in simple, one-sentence prayers, submit your requests to God and close by thanking God for his commitment to your relationship with him and how he has used this session to teach you more about dependence on him. Pray also for the hearts of those God revealed to you during the Circles of Life exercise on page 32.

14. Between group meetings, use the Reflections verses provided at the end of each session in your quiet time. Each day read the daily verse(s) and give prayerful consideration to what you learn about God, his Spirit, and his place in your life. Then record your thoughts, insights, or prayer in the space provided.

STUDY NOTES

Pharisees. This major sect of Judaism taught that only the most righteous would experience immortality. To achieve this, the Pharisees taught a strict observance of the Law and a complete separation from the heathen. The name Pharisee actually means "separatists" though its original meaning had more to do with separating from the heathen during captivity during the time of Zerubbabel and Ezra. This stance of separation caused a great deal of conflict with Jesus' teaching and practices of interacting and socializing with "sinners."

Went up on the roof and lowered him. The roof was easily accessible through a set of stairs and was commonly used as a patio or workspace in the household. It was not uncommon for residents to access their roofs. Here Luke paints the picture of the paralytic's friends removing tiles from the roof (unlike the common view of a clay roof in a poorer Palestinian home) and lowering their friend through the opening.

Blasphemy? Who can forgive sins but God alone? In the Jewish view, forgiveness and judgment were reserved for God alone to declare in the final day. For Jesus to declare that the paralytic's sins were forgiven was to not only lay claim to a role reserved for God, but was also to bring forgiveness from the future into the present. By the standards of the Jewish leaders, this was nothing short of blasphemy.

Briefly share your prayer requests with the large group, making notations below. Then gather in small groups of two to four to pray for each other.

Date: _____

PRAYER REQUESTS

_____

_____

_____

_____

_____

_____

_____

_____

_____

_____

_____

PRAISE REPORT

_____

_____

_____

_____

_____

_____

_____

_____

REFLECTIONS

Each day read the daily verse(s) and give prayerful consideration to what you learn about God, his Spirit, and his place in your life. Then record your thoughts, insights, or prayer in the Reflect section. On day six record a summary of what you have learned over the entire week through this study.

DAY 1   *"When Jesus saw their faith, he said, 'Friend, your sins are forgiven.'"*
(Luke 5:20)

REFLECT: _____

_____

_____

_____

_____

_____

_____

_____

_____

DAY 2   *"Everyone was amazed and gave praise to God. They were filled with awe and said, 'We have seen remarkable things today.'" (Luke 5:26)*

REFLECT: _____

_____

_____

_____

_____

_____

_____

DAY 3   *"Carry each other's burdens, and in this way you will fulfill the law of Christ. If anyone thinks he is something when he is nothing, he deceives himself." (Galatians 6:2–3)*

REFLECT: _____

_____

_____

_____

_____

_____

_____

_____

_____

_____

_____

DAY 4   *"A new command I give you: Love one another. As I have loved you, so you must love one another. By this all men will know that you are my disciples, if you love one another." (John 13:34–35)*

REFLECT: _____

_____

_____

_____

_____

_____

_____

_____

_____

_____

_____

DAY 5   *"This is how we know what love is: Jesus Christ laid down his life for us. And we ought to lay down our lives for our brothers." (1 John 3:16)*

REFLECT: _____

_____

_____

_____

_____

_____

_____

_____

_____

_____

_____

_____

DAY 6   Use the following space to write any thoughts God has put in your heart and mind about the things discussed during session two and/or during your Reflections time this week.

SUMMARY: _____

_____

_____

_____

_____

_____

_____

_____

_____

_____

_____

GIDEON — "LESS IS MORE"

As a career speaker who has made a living ministering through personal appearances, I have numerous experiences of witnessing the power of God through my weakness. Too numerous to count, actually. In fact, it has gotten to be that if I am sick or I am emotionally challenged when I have to deliver a talk, I know what God is doing, and I go with great anticipation because I know this is going to be a special visitation.

God is always reducing us to show us that it is his power, not ours, that is accomplishing something for the kingdom.

When our second child was born, we were away from home and our daughter came unexpectedly, two months early. That necessitated finding a place for my wife and other child to stay while we monitored our little girl's progress. Normally terrified by responsibilities like this, and challenged by decisions, I reached down inside myself and found a vital resource of everything I needed. And I knew it wasn't me. It was almost exhilarating because I knew I was running directly on Spirit power.

At the same time I was continuing a ministry nearby, driving between engagements and the hospital to be there for my daughter and family. Late nights, early mornings, emotional ups and downs — yet I sensed God's power in my messages that week more than ever. For me — and, I believe, for the people I served — this was special. Less is always more in God's economy.

CONNECTING WITH GOD'S FAMILY   20 MIN.

1. Welcome any newcomers joining the group today and take time to introduce yourselves. Then work through the following questions.

   Have you ever felt that God had something he wanted to teach you, show you, or accomplish through you at a time when you knew you were at your weakest — a time when you felt completely inadequate to do something you knew you should do? What did you do?

What were the barriers to overcome in the process of following through?

If you chose *not* to step out in faith in spite of your weakness, what was the result of that decision?

Finally, what did you learn through this experience?

2. Check in with your spiritual partner. Share any progress you made toward the goal you set for yourself in session two (the WHAT question on your Health Plan).

GROWING TO BE LIKE CHRIST   40 MIN.

The story of Gideon is one of God's power realized through human weakness. It took place at a time when judges ruled the nation of Israel, when God periodically rescued them from the hands of pagan nations they had fallen prey to due to disobedience. God purposely put Gideon in a position to attack an army too numerous to count with only 300 warriors of his own, and he gave them the strangest weapons: a torch inside a vessel and a horn. These 300 men on horseback completely surrounded their enemy, camped in a valley, and on command they smashed their vessels, held up their torches, blew their horns, and shouted, "For the sword of the Lord and Gideon!" The Midianites awoke to the sound of horns blowing from the surrounding hills, the shouts of warriors, and lights descending upon them from every angle. Thinking they were surrounded by legions of attacking troops, they killed many of their own men in the confusion of darkness before Gideon and his men ever reached them. Gideon then chased the remainder until he captured their leaders. That day, 120,000 swordsmen fell at the hand of Gideon and his little band of 300 men.

As such, it is a story of reduction. God reduces—sometimes even strips us—of all our resources but himself. As Corrie ten Boom says: "You don't realize Christ is all you need until Christ is all you have." This is the theme of Gideon's story and the focus of this lesson.

Read Judges 6:11–16 (NASB):

> Then the angel of the LORD came and sat under the oak that was in Ophrah, which belonged to Joash the Abiezrite as his son Gideon was beating out wheat in the wine press in order to save it from the Midianites. [12]The angel of the LORD appeared to him and said to him, "The LORD is with you, O valiant warrior."
>
> [13]Then Gideon said to him, "O my lord, if the LORD is with us, why then has all this happened to us? And where are all His miracles which our fathers told us about, saying, 'Did not the LORD bring us up from Egypt?' But now the LORD has abandoned us and given us into the hand of Midian." [14]The LORD looked at him and said, "Go in this your strength and deliver Israel from the hand of Midian. Have I not sent you?"
>
> [15]He said to Him, "O Lord, how shall I deliver Israel? Behold, my family is the least in Manasseh, and I am the youngest in my father's house." [16]But the LORD said to him, "Surely I will be with you, and you shall defeat Midian as one man."

3. Where did the angel of the Lord find Gideon? What was he doing there? What was his attitude at the time?

4. What excuses did Gideon give to avoid doing the work of the Lord? What excuses are common with people today? How do our "excuses" compare with Gideon's?

5. "If the Lord is with us, why then has all this happened to us?" Here is undoubtedly the most often asked question for believers and unbelievers alike. The unbelieving version is: If there is a God, why doesn't he do something about all the evil and injustice in the world? The Christian version is: Why does God allow bad things to happen to good people? How do you answer this question?

6. Why did the angel call Gideon a "valiant warrior"? What does God call you?

Read Judges 7:2 – 7 (NASB):

The LORD said to Gideon, "The people who are with you are too many for Me to give Midian into their hands, for Israel would become boastful, saying, 'My own power has delivered me.' ³Now therefore come, proclaim in the hearing of the people, saying, 'Whoever is afraid and trembling, let him return and depart from Mount Gilead.'" So 22,000 people returned, but 10,000 remained.

⁴Then the LORD said to Gideon, "The people are still too many; bring them down to the water and I will test them for you there. Therefore it shall be that he of whom I say to you, 'This one shall go with you,' he shall go with you; but everyone of whom I say to you, 'This one shall not go with you,' he shall not go." ⁵So he brought the people down to the water. And the LORD said to Gideon, "You shall separate everyone who laps the water with his tongue as a dog laps, as well as everyone who kneels to drink."

⁶Now the number of those who lapped, putting their hand to their mouth, was 300 men; but all the rest of the people kneeled to drink water. ⁷The LORD said to Gideon, "I will deliver you with the 300 men who lapped and will give the Midianites into your hands; so let all the other people go, each man to his home."

7. God took charge of Gideon's army and reduced it so that Israel would *know* that their victory was by his power. Have you ever fallen into thinking it was your own power and not God's that you had to depend on? A few of you share a time when relying on God's power helped you succeed. How did you know that it was God's power, and not your own, that ensured your success?

Read Judges 7:19–22 (NASB):

So Gideon and the hundred men who were with him came to the outskirts of the camp at the beginning of the middle watch, when they had just posted the watch; and they blew the trumpets and smashed the pitchers that were in their hands.

20When the three companies blew the trumpets and broke the pitchers, they held the torches in their left hands and the trumpets in their right hands for blowing, and cried, "A sword for the LORD and for Gideon!"

21Each stood in his place around the camp; and all the army ran, crying out as they fled.

22When they blew 300 trumpets, the LORD set the sword of one against another even throughout the whole army; and the army fled as far as Beth-shittah toward Zererah, as far as the edge of Abel-meholah, by Tabbath.

8. In 2 Corinthians 4:7, Paul states: "But we have this treasure in jars of clay to show that this all-surpassing power is from God and not from us." Given that the treasure he refers to is most likely "the light of the knowledge of the glory of God in the face of Christ" from the previous verse, how does this

picture echo the story of Gideon? What has to happen to the vessel for the light to shine? What happens to us?

9. Have you ever before considered that it is God's presence in our human weakness that actually makes our ministry powerful? Write what you learn after each reference below.

Matthew 28:17

Romans 8:11–12

Philippians 4:13

Colossians 1:27

What can stand in the way of this?

10. How would you characterize Gideon after this event as compared to before? (Scan the rest of Judges 7 and Judges 8.) What characteristics are built in us by acting in faith? How can we encourage each other to believe God and step out in faith?

FOR DEEPER STUDY

Gideon's timidity shows when he asks three times for a sign from God (Judges 6:17, 36–40) and God grants his requests. And as if that wasn't enough, God added a sign of his own by allowing Gideon to overhear someone in the enemy camp interpreting a dream to mean that the Israelites were going to be victorious over them (7:9–15). What does this show about the nature of God?

How has God helped you overcome your fear of believing and stepping out in faith?

In 2 Corinthians 3:12–13, Paul uses Moses as an example of timidity and fear but also reveals a reason why Moses wore a veil over his face. Do we not do the same thing when trusting our own strength and ingenuity? What methods do we use to hide the fact that our clever tricks are not working?

In 2 Corinthians 3:18, Paul paints a picture of Christ's character being built in us all: "And we, who with unveiled faces all reflect the Lord's glory, are being transformed into his likeness with ever-increasing glory, which comes from the Lord, who is the Spirit." This is a process that we share together, but it only happens with unveiled faces. As we have the commitment and the courage to walk this way together, God will build character in us as we look to him. That's a promise.

DEVELOPING YOUR GIFTS TO SERVE OTHERS   10 MIN.

11. In Judges 6:36–40 we see Gideon questioning his own ability to hear God's instruction. Yet God proved his faithfulness as Gideon took small steps of obedience and became God's valiant warrior. What step of obedience or area of trust do

you need to address in order to fully develop your ability to serve God?

12. As a group, take a few minutes to discuss a project or ministry you could serve in together to meet a need in your church or community. Spend some time in prayer asking God to show you the needs around you and how this group can meet those needs. Brainstorm ideas now, and someone volunteer to research other ideas and/or ask your pastor or someone else in leadership at your church about any unmet needs your group could meet.

In addition, you may know members of your church who are ill, in a nursing home, jobless, or in some other situation that requires extra care. You may have a neighbor who could use a batch of cookies, or your church may have a ministry to the poor. You are the church — your pastor can't do everything! And while pastors routinely make hospital visits (for example), you can't imagine how it affects someone when a whole group shows up in his hospital room.

Keep it simple and assign someone to plan it over the course of the next few weeks. You'll find the entire process, from start to finish, to be a great bonding experience. Also, write down your group's service project on your Personal Health Plan on page 100. Be prepared to report the status of this planned effort during session four of this study.

 SHARING YOUR LIFE MISSION EVERY DAY   10 MIN.

13. Turn to the Circles of Life exercise on page 32 and review the names you listed there. How did your invitations go this past week? Share with the group some of the responses you received when you invited people to join your small group. Talk about what the responses might mean. (If anyone joined the group this week in response to an invitation, tell why you decided to come.)

If you haven't yet had the opportunity to make the invitations, plan to do it within the next forty-eight hours.

SURRENDERING YOUR LIFE FOR GOD'S PLEASURE   15–20 MIN.

14. Share your prayer requests now. Write down group members' prayer requests on the Prayer and Praise Report provided on page 48. Then divide into circles of two to four for the prayer time. Close your time together by praying for the needs expressed today by group members, and remember to pray for the people listed in your Circles of Life on page 32. As God answers your prayer requests, be sure to celebrate how he is working among and through your group.

15. Use the Reflections verses at the end of this session in your quiet time this week. Record any thoughts or direction you receive from the Lord in the space provided.

STUDY NOTES

The angel of the Lord. This appearance is regarded as a theophany, an actual representation of God himself in a visible human form.

Joash the Abiezrite. Abiezer was a family of the tribe of Manasseh. According to Judges 6:15, it was a small family: "the least of Manasseh."

Midianites. The Midianites were descendents of Midian, the fourth son of Abraham by Keturah (Genesis 25:1–2). At the time of Gideon, the Midianites had united with the Amalekites and oppressed the Israelites not so much by military might, but by overrunning the grain harvest (Judges 6:1–6). While the Israelites were not in captivity per se, the Midianites' actions brought the Israelites to the brink of extinction.

The army fled as far as Beth-shittah ... edge of Abel-meholah. Beth-shittah literally means "place of the acacia" and is an unknown location only mentioned in this passage. Abel-meholah was located in the northern part of the Jordan valley.

Briefly share your prayer requests with the large group, making notations below. Then gather in small groups of two to four to pray for each other.

Date: _____

PRAYER REQUESTS

_____

_____

_____

_____

_____

_____

_____

_____

_____

_____

_____

_____

PRAISE REPORT

_____

_____

_____

_____

_____

_____

_____

_____

REFLECTIONS

Each day read the daily verse(s) and give prayerful consideration to what you learn about God, his Spirit, and his place in your life. Then record your thoughts, insights, or prayer in the Reflect section. On day six record a summary of what you have learned over the entire week through this study.

DAY 1   *"The Lord said to Gideon, 'You have too many men for me to deliver Midian into their hands. In order that Israel may not boast against me that her own strength has saved her . . .'"* (Judges 7:2)

REFLECT: _____

_____

_____

_____

_____

_____

_____

_____

_____

DAY 2   *"But we have this treasure in jars of clay to show that this all-surpassing power is from God and not from us."* (2 Corinthians 4:7)

REFLECT: _____

_____

_____

_____

_____

_____

_____

_____

_____

DAY 3   *"Therefore, since we have such a hope, we are very bold." (2 Corinthians 3:12)*

REFLECT: _____

_____

_____

_____

_____

_____

_____

_____

_____

_____

_____

_____

DAY 4   *"And we, who with unveiled faces all reflect the Lord's glory, are being transformed into his likeness with ever-increasing glory, which comes from the Lord, who is the Spirit." (2 Corinthians 3:18)*

REFLECT: _____

_____

_____

_____

_____

_____

_____

_____

_____

_____

DAY 5   *"I have given them the glory that you gave me, that they may be one as we are one." (John 17:22)*

REFLECT: _____

_____

_____

_____

_____

_____

_____

_____

_____

_____

_____

_____

DAY 6   Use the following space to write any thoughts God has put in your heart and mind about the things discussed during session three and/ or during your Reflections time this week.

REFLECT: _____

_____

_____

_____

_____

_____

_____

_____

_____

_____

_____

_____

SESSION 4
JOHN THE BAPTIST— "BEST MAN"

For a number of years, I attended a conference for people in my line of ministry put on by an organization that sought to help us be better at what we do. The event was at a beautiful resort in the Rocky Mountains, and every year the sponsor brought in a couple with the gift of hospitality to do nothing but cook and create a warm, homey environment in one of the cabins, where conferees could come, relax, and spend quality time together.

I think back on those years and all the famous people I met who are now a blur in my mind, but the ones who stand out are the Fabers, that couple who worked so hard to give us some very special memories. Some nights we were up talking and praying until the wee hours of the morning, yet after an hour or two of sleep, our hosts were up cooking and getting ready for another day. Not only did they provide hospitality, they provided conversation, advice, and, most of all, love.

I'm sure the Fabers are just two in a very long list of unsung heroes who will be honored in heaven. People who did what they were asked to do, asked no questions, and claimed no attention. The amazing thing about them was that they didn't require any of these things. It's not that they sacrificed for this. They served joyfully, satisfied and fulfilled in what God gave them to do.

CONNECTING WITH GOD'S FAMILY   20 MIN.

Welcome any newcomers who have joined the group this week and spend some time introducing yourselves.

In this session, we will focus on the kind of character required to be a servant. What it takes to play second fiddle. It's a pretty radical departure to seek out this kind of role when the overwhelming majority of all our attention in this culture is placed on being top dog. It's dog-eat-dog in a zero-sum, winner-takes-all game. And along comes Jesus, who will himself choose servanthood as his mode of operation. And Jesus is introduced to us by John the Baptist, who is more than happy to give his spotlight away to Jesus.

If people are serving, they are, of necessity, in community. You can't serve without having someone to serve. Serving always puts you in the context of others, because its overall focus is always other-oriented. Being number one is self-serving; being number two or lower is to be in community with those you serve. (And don't forget, if you feel compelled to give yourself a high number here, that the last shall be first in the kingdom of heaven.)

1. What characteristics make up a servant, or to put it another way, if you were interviewing someone to serve you, what qualities would you look for?

2. Pair up with your spiritual partner and turn to your Personal Health Plan (pages 100–101). Share with your partner your progress in working on the goal you set in session two. What obstacles hindered you from following through? Then, review your Personal Health Assessments together and identify any additional areas you want to work on to enhance your spiritual growth. Share any new goals with your partner so that they can continue to hold you accountable as you grow throughout this study. Make a note about yours and your partner's progress and how you can pray for each other this week.

3. Take some time now to discuss what is next for your group. Will you be staying together for another study? What will your next study be? Turn to the Small Group Agreement on pages 97–98 and talk about any changes you would like to make in your group as you move forward.

GROWING TO BE LIKE CHRIST   40 MIN.

John the Baptist had actually been in the spotlight for a while, baptizing all who came out to him, and to do so they had to trek into the wilderness to find him. "People went out to him from Jerusalem and all Judea and the whole region of the Jordan. Confessing their sins, they were baptized by him in the Jordan River" (Matthew 3:5–6). Something was up. A steady stream had been coming. God was preparing people and, for a while, John was the guy getting all the attention. Yet all along, he knew that he was to play only a supporting role in the grand scheme of things.

As you may know, John was a controversial character who is famous for being a nonconformist, living in the desert, wearing camel skin, and eating a steady diet of locusts and honey. And though he was a great prophet in his own right — even believed by some to be the reincarnation of the Old Testament Elijah; Jesus himself called him "the Elijah who was to come" (Matthew 11:14) — he knew all along that his primary role was to prepare the way for the one who was to come after him — one whose sandals he considered himself unfit to carry (3:11).

In the following account from John's gospel, John the Baptist calls himself the "friend who attends the bridegroom" — the bridegroom being Christ and the bride, his church. That would make John the Baptist the best man. Is it any wonder that Christ's first miracle was performed at a wedding?

Read John 3:22–30:

> *After this, Jesus and his disciples went out into the Judean countryside, where he spent some time with them, and baptized. ²³Now John also was baptizing at Aenon near Salim, because there was plenty of water, and people were constantly coming to be baptized. ²⁴(This was before John was put in prison.) ²⁵An argument developed between some of John's disciples and a certain Jew over the matter of ceremonial washing. ²⁶They came to John and said to him, "Rabbi, that man who was with you on the other side of the Jordan — the one you testified about — well, he is baptizing, and everyone is going to him."*
>
> *²⁷To this John replied, "A man can receive only what is given him from heaven. ²⁸You yourselves can testify that I said, 'I am not the Christ but am sent ahead of him.' ²⁹The bride belongs to the bridegroom. The friend who attends the bridegroom waits and listens for him, and is full of joy when he hears the bridegroom's voice. That joy is mine, and it is now complete. ³⁰He must become greater; I must become less."*

John was pretty powerful in his own right. He had his moment of glory. He even had his own disciples. Yet John was about to give up all of this. He wasn't even going to share the stage; he was going to get off the stage and allow himself to be relegated to a bit part in the unfolding drama, ultimately losing his head over something as obscure as poking his nose into King Herod's business.

Yet upon hearing of his death, Jesus would proclaim, "I tell you, among those born of women there is no one greater than John" (Luke 7:28).

4. With all this attention and accolades from Jesus himself, how did John see himself? If there is no one born of woman greater than John, what does that say of us?

5. Have you ever been in the spotlight? Have you ever had your own moment of glory? What did you do with it?

6. Bono, lead singer for the Irish rock band U2 and arguably the most popular and most powerful rock celebrity since Elvis, has a tradition he established in all U2's concerts of taking a hand-held spotlight off the floor and shining it all over his audience. It was symbolic of taking the spotlight off himself and reflecting it on someone else, making his audience, for a moment in time, the real star of the show. How do we turn attention to Christ without drawing attention to ourselves?

7. Jesus was not the only one with disciples. John's disciples came with questions from John and they also came bearing the news of John's death. Jesus' disciples had disciples of their own (for example, Paul had Timothy). How about you? Do you have any disciples? Should you?

Read Matthew 11:7–9:

As John's disciples were leaving [after questioning Jesus about his identity], Jesus began to speak to the crowd about John: "What did you go out into the desert to see? A reed swayed by the wind? ⁸If not, what did you go out to see? A man dressed in fine clothes? No, those who wear fine clothes are in kings' palaces. ⁹Then what did you go out to see? A prophet? Yes, I tell you, and more than a prophet."

8. This portrait of John the Baptist reveals an incredible strength of character. This was not a man to be bought or placated by anyone. This was a prophet who said what God wanted him to say regardless of the consequences (the final consequence being his head on a platter). No one threatened or intimidated him, King Herod included. How do you differentiate between this strong character portrait painted by Jesus and John's own view of himself (John 3:28–30)? How can these two coexist? In what area of your life of faith do you need to develop a backbone like John?

9. What do you think it means to wait and listen for the bridegroom's voice? How does that build character in us?

10. John the Baptist was a true servant of God. He was born for it. But most of us, though we are all called to serve, don't have such a confident view of our calling. Who are you serving?

FOR DEEPER STUDY

In Matthew 11:14 Jesus says of John the Baptist, "If you are willing to accept it, he is the Elijah who was to come." Who was he talking to here, and why would they have a difficult time accepting this? (Check back to the opening verses of Matthew 11.)

The Elijah Jesus was speaking about was predicted in the last two verses of the Old Testament. "See, I will send you the prophet Elijah before that great and dreadful day of the LORD comes. He will turn the hearts of the fathers to their children, and the hearts of the children to their fathers; or else I will come and strike the land with a curse" (Malachi 4:5–6). Did you ever notice that the Old Testament ends with a prediction that the opening lines of the New Testament story fulfills? John's role was to spearhead a revival that would accompany the outbreak of the ministry of the Son of God. It's only natural that the coming of Christ would be preceded by a spiritual renewal that would turn people's hearts back to the right things. Why do you suppose the prophecy singles out the hearts of children and their fathers?

When God wants to change people, he changes their hearts. Jeremiah predicted this as the new covenant, and Jesus affirmed it when, at the Last Supper, he had his disciples drink from the new covenant in his blood—that would be won by his death. "'This is the covenant I will make with the house of Israel after that time,' declares the LORD. 'I will put my law in their minds and write it on their hearts. I will be their God, and they will be my people'" (Jeremiah 31:33). The old covenant tries to get us to act right based on an external standard; the new covenant promises a new heart and mind so we can both interpret what God wants us to do, and actually want to do it ourselves.

Has anyone in your group ever tried to quit a bad habit? You probably found out that the hardest part is wanting to quit. There are all kinds of programs and helps for those who want to quit something, but what about those who know they should, but don't want to?

Sin is just like that. We know we should stop but we don't want to. This is why we need a new heart that is turned toward God. It's only as we rely on that new heart that any lasting change can be produced in our lives.

 ## DEVELOPING YOUR GIFTS TO SERVE OTHERS   10 MIN.

11. Engage in a practical and fun exercise called "secret servants." On slips of paper, have each person write his or her name and (optionally) one personal need. Put all the names in a hat, and let everyone draw out a name. You will be that person's "secret servant" for one week. (If you get your name or your spouse's, draw another name.) Respond to that person's need, or ask God to show you how to serve that person in a simple, creative way.

Right here in this group is a great place to begin developing a servant's heart. People in your group may have all sorts of needs, such as:

- Child care during meetings or at other times

- Transportation

- Help finding a job

- Emotional or practical support while caring for an aging or ill relative

- Practical help when a friend or family member is hospitalized
- Encouragement and prayer in the face of trials
- Help with household tasks during a busy season of life
- Companionship during loneliness or loss

12. In session three we asked you to look for a project or ministry you could participate in together as a group. Update the group on what you found out. Finalize any plans needed to make this service in your community a reality.

SHARING YOUR LIFE MISSION EVERY DAY   10 MIN.

John the Baptist gave himself completely to serving the Lord to meet the need of those he would bring into eternity with him. At times a small act of service can change a person's responsiveness to hearing the gospel.

13. What are some things that prevent people from giving themselves selflessly to those who do not know the Lord? Who do you know that you could begin to serve in some small way?

SURRENDERING YOUR LIFE FOR GOD'S PLEASURE   15–20 MIN.

John the Baptist gave his life fully in the service of God— standing up for truth. His life exemplifies total surrender. Each of you share one thing you need to surrender to God today. In your prayer time, pray that God will help you surrender these things to him.

14. One way to show your love for one another is to continually pray for each other's needs. Share any needs and pray together before you close your time today. Use the Prayer and Praise Report on page 62 to record your requests and any praises the group has. Commit to praying for each other daily between now and your next group meeting.

15. Use the Reflections verses at the end of this session in your quiet time this week. Record any thoughts or direction you receive from the Lord in the space provided.

STUDY NOTES

Aenon. Meaning "springs," Aenon may have been near the upper source of the Wady Far'ah, an open valley extending from Mount Ebal to the Jordan that is full of springs. A place has been found called Ainun, four miles north of the springs (Christiananswers.net).

Ceremonial washing. The Jews of the time had a very complicated and legalistic system of ritual washings. Some ceremonial washings were dictated in the Law related to the temple. Other rules were passed down through tradition.

Briefly share your prayer requests with the large group, making notations below. Then gather in small groups of two to four to pray for each other.

Date: _____

PRAYER REQUESTS

_____

_____

_____

_____

_____

_____

_____

_____

_____

_____

PRAISE REPORT

_____

_____

_____

_____

_____

_____

_____

_____

_____

REFLECTIONS

Each day read the daily verse(s) and give prayerful consideration to what you learn about God, his Spirit, and his place in your life. Then record your thoughts, insights, or prayer in the Reflect section. On day six record a summary of what you have learned over the entire week through this study.

DAY 1   *"People went out to him from Jerusalem and all Judea and the whole region of the Jordan. Confessing their sins, they were baptized by him in the Jordan River." (Matthew 3:5–6)*

REFLECT: _____

_____

_____

_____

_____

_____

_____

_____

_____

_____

DAY 2   *" 'You are Israel's teacher,' " said Jesus, 'and do you not understand these things?' " (John 3:10)*

REFLECT: _____

_____

_____

_____

_____

_____

_____

_____

DAY 3 *"To this John replied, 'A man can receive only what is given him from heaven.'"* (John 3:27)

REFLECT: _____

_____

_____

_____

_____

_____

_____

_____

_____

_____

_____

DAY 4 *"You yourselves can testify that I said, 'I am not the Christ but am sent ahead of him.'"* (John 3:28)

REFLECT: _____

_____

_____

_____

_____

_____

_____

_____

_____

_____

DAY 5   *"See, I will send you the prophet Elijah before that great and dreadful day of the LORD comes. He will turn the hearts of the fathers to their children, and the hearts of the children to their fathers; or else I will come and strike the land with a curse." (Malachi 4:5–6)*

REFLECT: _____

_____

_____

_____

_____

_____

_____

_____

_____

_____

_____

DAY 6   Use the following space to write any thoughts God has put in your heart and mind about the things discussed during session four and/or during your Reflections time this week.

REFLECT: _____

_____

_____

_____

_____

_____

_____

_____

_____

_____

_____

JONAH— WHAT *NOT* TO DO

I n an amazing true story that took place in Atlanta in March 2005, a single mom survived an all-night ordeal being held hostage by a man who had, on a rampage, allegedly just killed a judge and three other people. The remarkable thing about the story was that the woman, Ashley Smith, was herself in the process of reconnecting with her own faith when she was used by God to turn her captor's life around. In the course of one night, he came to his senses, realized that there was hope in Christ, and turned himself in.

What continues to be remarkable about this story is not so much Ashley's heroic actions as it was her ordinary ones. At the time she was reading *The Purpose Driven® Life* by Rick Warren and she simply picked up the next chapter and started reading it to him. Someone has said that a person leading someone to Christ is like one beggar telling another beggar where the food is. I can't think of a better example of that than this.

This should give us all hope and allow us to forever bury the myth that says you can't minister to someone until you have reached some spiritual plateau yourself. You minister out of who you are and where you are in your own journey. Ashley Smith merely took what she was receiving and shared it with someone else. It's not any different for any one of us, from the mature Christian to the new one.

CONNECTING WITH GOD'S FAMILY   20 MIN.

There's a story out about a girl in a Christian school who flunked witnessing. Certainly, we could all say there are times when we, too, have flunked witnessing. Either we didn't know what it was, or we knew, but didn't do anything about it.

Unfortunately, there is a lot of guilt and fear associated with sharing our faith with unbelievers. Sometimes it's strong enough to keep us from even trying.

1. A few of you tell of a time when you shared your faith with someone and they received Jesus. What are some characteristics that are common to all your stories?

Next, some of you recall a time when you shared your faith with someone but the message was rejected. What are some of the common characteristics of these stories?

Can you identify some characteristics that are common to all the stories?

2. Sit with your spiritual partner. Discuss the following question: What are your own personal obstacles to sharing your faith?

GROWING TO BE LIKE CHRIST   40 MIN.

Few Bible stories are more recognizable than that of Jonah, known by children and adults both inside and outside the church. What isn't as well known, however, are the subtleties inside the story. Some would come as a surprise to many. We will be looking at the story to find out how God sees unbelievers, and what we can learn from the shortcomings in Jonah's character.

Those of you who are parents are probably familiar with the Berenstain Bears book *The Bike Lesson* in which Papa bear teaches his son how to ride a bicycle by breaking every rule he is trying to teach. Each time he does this, he punctuates it by pointing out that what he just demonstrated was what *not* to do, "and let that be a lesson to you!" Jonah is a lesson on how *not* to witness, and how *not* to think about those who are yet unsaved.

Read Jonah 1:1–3:

> *The word of the LORD came to Jonah son of Amittai: ²"Go to the great city of Nineveh and preach against it, because its wickedness has come up before me." ³But Jonah ran away from the LORD and headed for Tarshish. He went down to Joppa, where he found a ship bound for that port. After paying the fare, he went aboard and sailed for Tarshish to flee from the LORD.*

3. Have you ever done this—run straight in the opposite direction of where you knew God wanted you? What happened?

Upon first read, it's easy to misinterpret why Jonah didn't want to go to Nineveh. God called him to preach against the city because of its wickedness. Well, just how popular is a guy who is coming down on everybody having a good time being wicked? Jonah would be familiar with prophets before him who had not been treated very favorably due to their unpopular messages from God. Anyone can understand why he might be reluctant to go. But at the end of this story, Jonah's real reason for not wanting to go to Nineveh is revealed, and it's a big surprise.

We pick up the story after Jonah's rescue from the sea, when he finally goes to Nineveh and proclaims God's warning about the destruction to come should the people not turn from their wickedness and worship the Lord. Well, lo and behold, they heed the warning. The message strikes fear into their hearts, they tear their clothes in anguish and remorse, and want to know what they must do to make amends.

Read Jonah 3:10–4:3:

> *When God saw what they [the Ninevites] did and how they turned from their evil ways, he had compassion and did not bring upon them the destruction he had threatened.*

4:1But Jonah was greatly displeased and became angry. 2He prayed to the LORD, "O LORD, is this not what I said when I was still at home? That is why I was so quick to flee to Tarshish. I knew that you are a gracious and compassionate God, slow to anger and abounding in love, a God who relents from sending calamity. 3Now, O LORD, take away my life, for it is better for me to die than to live."

There it is. Jonah didn't want to go to Nineveh because he had a premonition that they would respond favorably to his preaching and repent from their wicked ways. And God, because he's so gracious and compassionate, would change his mind about bringing destruction on the city.

Reading between the lines, here is what we get: Jonah wanted the city to burn. He wanted to go in there and bomb the place with predictions of God's judgment, then sit back and watch God's wrath rain down from heaven.

4. Nineveh was an enemy of Israel and Jonah didn't want God to show them any mercy. Look back at Jonah 3:10. What does this verse tell you about God's attitude toward the Ninevites?

Reflect on your own life. Is there anyone who has wronged you, or really makes you angry for some reason, that you are holding a grudge against? Someone that you find it difficult or impossible to have compassion for? We tend to rationalize that these feelings are okay to have because (1) maybe they're not Christians who are hell bound anyway or (2) they wronged you and don't deserve your compassion or forgiveness. But we can see from Jonah 3:10 that this is not a biblical response. God gives compassion and forgiveness to anyone who repents and turns to him. What can we do to show compassion and forgiveness to even the most difficult of people?

70

Read 2 Corinthians 5:18-20:

All this is from God, who reconciled us to himself through Christ and gave us the ministry of reconciliation: ¹⁹that God was reconciling the world to himself in Christ, not counting men's sins against them. And he has committed to us the message of reconciliation. ²⁰We are therefore Christ's ambassadors, as though God were making his appeal through us. We implore you on Christ's behalf: Be reconciled to God.

5. These should be very encouraging words to those who are afraid to witness: the purpose of sharing Christ with people is so that they might experience the graciousness and compassion of God. Our news is all good news. The wrath of God has already been poured out on his Son (on the cross) so that his grace and mercy may be bestowed upon us. What does it mean that Christ is not counting men's sins against them?

6. Where does the need for justice and revenge fall in relation to one's character development? In other words, would you expect a younger Christian or a more mature one to be caught up in the attitudes of Jonah? Why?

   What does time teach you about how you see others in relation to yourself?

7. It appears that Jonah didn't really learn a lot from spending three days inside the belly of a great fish and getting a new lease on life. He still remained the reluctant prophet. God had mercy on him by saving him from sure death in the sea,

but Jonah didn't seem to be that grateful (Jonah 4:3). Otherwise, he would have been more compassionate toward the Ninevites. What does this tell us about character development? Is suffering and hardship always going to produce a more proven character, or is there some requirement from us before this usefulness and growth can come out of our situations? What was Jonah missing?

FOR DEEPER STUDY

The Scripture says that after Jonah finished preaching, he went to a place outside the city and waited to see what would happen. He became angry and depressed. While he waited, God caused a vine to grow up over where Jonah sat and it gave him protection from the sun, "and Jonah was very happy about the vine" (Jonah 4:6). But the next day, God withered the vine and the sun came up and bore down on Jonah causing a mild case of heat stroke (verses 7–8). He wanted to die.

> But God said to Jonah, "Do you have a right to be angry about the vine?" "I do," he said. "I am angry enough to die."

> [10]But the LORD said, "You have been concerned about this vine, though you did not tend it or make it grow. It sprang up overnight and died overnight. [11]But Nineveh has more than a hundred and twenty thousand people who cannot tell their right hand from their left, and many cattle as well. Should I not be concerned about that great city?"

Jonah had nothing to do with the plant growing and withering. There is a lesson here for us. We have nothing to do with the soul of another person—what makes them receptive to the gospel or not. We also have nothing to do with the ultimate destiny of another person—who will grow and who will wither.

If we don't have any control over the responses to our sharing of the gospel, what do we have control over?

God said that the people of Nineveh couldn't tell their right hand from their left hand. He's not talking about lack of intelligence. It's not that they were stupid; it's that they were not morally conscious. They had no sense of what was right and what was wrong. Paul says in Romans 7:23 that everyone has a law within them (a conscience), and that if they listen to it, they could discover the first elemental steps in knowing God. But if you ignore your conscience, over time, it no longer speaks to you. You become detached from any moral judgment.

This is similar to Christ's assessment from the cross in regard to the people who were beating and killing him: "Father, forgive them, for they do not know what they are doing" (Luke 23:34).

It appears that in both these cases, God is cutting people some very serious slack. Does this mean that people aren't responsible for their sins?

What does this mean for us in our attitude toward unbelievers?

DEVELOPING YOUR GIFTS TO SERVE OTHERS   15–20 MIN.

As God's children, we need to build each other up, supporting each other in the work God has for us.

8. One way to affirm and encourage each other is to do the "hot seat" exercise. Set a chair in the center of the room. Select an individual in your group to be in the "hot seat." Pass out half sheets of paper or index cards to each group member. Have each group member write, "This is what I've learned to appreciate about you" or "This is what I've learned to value in you," followed by something specifically appreciated or valued

about the person in the "hot seat." Only a phrase or sentence is needed. When everyone has finished writing, pass all the sheets to one group member to read aloud to the individual. Repeat this process for every member of your group.

9. Take some time now to finalize your plans for a social event following the completion of this study. Planning socials in between studies gives you a break, builds relationships in your group, and helps you get to know each other better. Plan what you will do, when you will do it, and where it will be. It does not have to be elaborate; it could be just a potluck or barbecue. You might even want to invite some unbelieving friends, just so they can see a believing community enjoying life together.

 SHARING YOUR LIFE MISSION EVERY DAY   5 MIN.

10. Is there someone in your life who you don't really care to spend time with who doesn't know the Lord? Maybe you don't really think you are called to share Jesus with them. Commit to praying for that person every day until you see a change in them or in your attitude toward them. Begin to look for signs of God's work.

 SURRENDERING YOUR LIFE FOR GOD'S PLEASURE   15 MIN.

11. To Jonah, the graciousness and compassion of God is a bummer. Under what circumstances might someone think the same thing? Spend some time in prayer thanking God for his graciousness and compassion, first toward us, and then toward others.

12. The next session is the last for this study. We have suggested the possibility of serving Communion. *Consider whether or not this is appropriate for your group at this time.* If so, make plans before you leave today. In the appendix on pages 106–107 you will find instructions for serving Communion.

13. After you have shared prayer requests, break up into subgroups of two to four to pray for one another's needs. Use the Prayer and Praise Report on page 76 to record prayer needs.

Commit to praying faithfully for one another at the same time each day throughout the next week. Consider sending an email or note at least once during the week to encourage each other.

14. Use the Reflections verses at the end of this session in your quiet time this week. Record any thoughts or direction you receive from the Lord in the space provided.

STUDY NOTES

Son of Amittai. The father of Jonah was from the tribe of Zebulun and was a native of Gath Hepher (2 Kings 14:25).

Nineveh. Founded by Nimrod (Genesis 10:8–10), this city sat on the eastern bank of the Tigris River opposite the modern city of Mosul in modern-day Iraq. Nineveh was a major city in the Assyrian empire.

Tarshish. Tarshish was a well-known port city in Old Testament times. References to "the fleet of Tarshish" appear in several passages (1 Kings 10:22; 22:48; 2 Chronicles 9:21). The city was also known as Tarsus in Cilicia in Asia Minor or Tarsisi in Assyrian records.

Joppa. Joppa was located about thirty miles northwest of Jerusalem. Today, Joppa is the modern city of Yafo or Tel Aviv-Yafo.

Briefly share your prayer requests with the large group, making notations below. Then gather in small groups of two to four to pray for each other.

Date: _____

PRAYER REQUESTS

_____

_____

_____

_____

_____

_____

_____

_____

_____

_____

_____

PRAISE REPORT

_____

_____

_____

_____

_____

_____

_____

_____

REFLECTIONS

Each day read the daily verse(s) and give prayerful consideration to what you learn about God, his Spirit, and his place in your life. Then record your thoughts, insights, or prayer in the Reflect section. On day six record a summary of what you have learned over the entire week through this study.

DAY 1 *"When God saw what they did and how they turned from their evil ways, he had compassion and did not bring upon them the destruction he had threatened." (Jonah 3:10)*

REFLECT: _____

_____

_____

_____

_____

_____

_____

_____

_____

DAY 2 *"I knew that you are a gracious and compassionate God, slow to anger and abounding in love, a God who relents from sending calamity." (Jonah 4:2b)*

REFLECT: _____

_____

_____

_____

_____

_____

_____

_____

_____

DAY 3   *"All this is from God, who reconciled us to himself through Christ and gave us the ministry of reconciliation: that God was reconciling the world to himself in Christ, not counting men's sins against them. And he has committed to us the message of reconciliation. We are therefore Christ's ambassadors, as though God were making his appeal through us. We implore you on Christ's behalf: Be reconciled to God." (2 Corinthians 5:18–20)*

REFLECT: _____

_____

_____

_____

_____

_____

_____

_____

_____

_____

DAY 4   *"But I see another law at work in the members of my body, waging war against the law of my mind and making me a prisoner of the law of sin at work within my members." (Romans 7:23)*

REFLECT: _____

_____

_____

_____

_____

_____

_____

_____

_____

DAY 5   *"Jesus said, 'Father, forgive them, for they do not know what they are doing.' And they divided up his clothes by casting lots." (Luke 23:34)*

REFLECT: _____

_____

_____

_____

_____

_____

_____

_____

_____

_____

_____

_____

DAY 6   Use the following space to write any thoughts God has put in your heart and mind about the things discussed during session five and/or during your Reflections time this week.

SUMMARY: _____

_____

_____

_____

_____

_____

_____

_____

_____

_____

_____

_____

SESSION 6

A SINFUL WOMAN — TRUE WORSHIP

I saw a movie a while back in which a seasoned salesman, Phil, is lecturing a young greenhorn, Bob, about character and where it comes from. He tells Bob that he does not possess any real character to speak of because he hasn't lived long enough to regret anything.

Bob protests: "You mean I have to go out and do something I will regret in order to have character?"

"No, Bob," replies Phil. "I'm saying you've already done plenty of things to regret, you just don't know what they are. It's when you discover them, when you see the folly in something you've done, and you wish that you had it to do over, but you know you can't, because it's too late. So you pick that thing up, and carry it with you to remind you that life goes on, the world will spin without you, you really don't matter in the end. Then you will gain character, because honesty will reach out from inside and tattoo itself across your face."

This conversation cut deep into me when I first heard it and has resonated ever since. My problem with sin is much like Bob's was in this movie. I didn't think I had any—at least none to speak of, relative to everyone else's sinful lives. You see, I grew up in the church, accepted Christ at a young age, and always did what was expected of me. I was a model child, sure that God was going to bless me because of my good record. I can also remember staring into my thimbleful of grape juice during Communion, trying hard to feel something. Everyone around me seemed to be feeling so much. Like Bob, I had much to regret, I just didn't know what it was.

The honesty that will "tattoo itself across your face" and mine is facing our own inability to live up to God's standard, other people's expectations, and even the standard of our own conscience. And until you face that, you are not really a whole person. You are living a lie, as I did for some time. This lesson is all about facing that lie, the sin behind it, and discovering the overwhelming love and worship that springs from an honest-to-goodness forgiven heart.

CONNECTING WITH GOD'S FAMILY   20 MIN.

Philip Yancey loves to tell the story about a man in his church who is a recovering alcoholic and faithfully attends both church and his AA meetings. One day he shared with Yancey an observation he had made about how differently people react in these two settings. For instance, when he is late to church, he gets the distinct impression, by the looks and body language of those around him, that he isn't being quite as responsible as they are. In direct contrast, if he is late to an AA meeting, the meeting stops and everyone gets up and hugs him because they know he almost didn't make it, and they are so glad he chose them over his need for alcohol.

1. Undoubtedly someone in your group has had some experience in recovery. Talk about that experience and discuss your reactions to Philip Yancey's story. How has God's forgiveness and love impacted your recovery?

2. Take time in this final session to connect with your spiritual partner. What has God been showing you through the sessions of this study? Check in with each other about the progress you have made in your spiritual growth and talk about whether you might like to continue in your mentoring relationship outside your Bible study group.

GROWING TO BE LIKE CHRIST   40 MIN.

The sinful woman of Luke 7:36–50, who had heard Jesus preach and turned from her sin, came to him out of love so that she could be forgiven. Similarly, we all sin and need to be forgiven so we can recover from whatever it is that holds us back from truly worshiping God.

Read Luke 7:36–50:

> Now one of the Pharisees invited Jesus to have dinner with
> him, so he went to the Pharisee's house and reclined at the
> table. [37]When a woman who had lived a sinful life in that
> town learned that Jesus was eating at the Pharisee's house,
> she brought an alabaster jar of perfume, [38]and as she stood
> behind him at his feet weeping, she began to wet his feet with
> her tears. Then she wiped them with her hair, kissed them
> and poured perfume on them.

³⁹When the Pharisee who had invited him saw this, he said to himself, "If this man were a prophet, he would know who is touching him and what kind of woman she is—that she is a sinner." ⁴⁰Jesus answered him, "Simon, I have something to tell you." "Tell me, teacher," he said.

⁴¹"Two men owed money to a certain moneylender. One owed him five hundred denarii, and the other fifty. ⁴²Neither of them had the money to pay him back, so he canceled the debts of both. Now which of them will love him more?" ⁴³Simon replied, "I suppose the one who had the bigger debt canceled." "You have judged correctly," Jesus said.

⁴⁴Then he turned toward the woman and said to Simon, "Do you see this woman? I came into your house. You did not give me any water for my feet, but she wet my feet with her tears and wiped them with her hair. ⁴⁵You did not give me a kiss, but this woman, from the time I entered, has not stopped kissing my feet. ⁴⁶You did not put oil on my head, but she has poured perfume on my feet. ⁴⁷Therefore, I tell you, her many sins have been forgiven—for she loved much. But he who has been forgiven little loves little." ⁴⁸Then Jesus said to her, "Your sins are forgiven."

⁴⁹The other guests began to say among themselves, "Who is this who even forgives sins?" ⁵⁰Jesus said to the woman, "Your faith has saved you; go in peace."

3. Jesus said, "He who has been forgiven little loves little" (verse 47b). What do you think this means? How did the woman demonstrate this truth?

4. Jesus taught a very simple principle here: The deeper the knowledge of sin, the greater the love. Does anyone see a pattern of our behavior in church that might go against making this a way of life, and if so, what is it?

5. How can we recognize the sin in our lives? Can we go into a closet and do this, or do we also need others to see the depth and ramifications of our sin? How is confessing sin to others different than confessing sin privately to God?

6. What was this sinful woman's form of worship? What emotions and acts of affection did it include?

Do we have anything in our practice of worship—both singularly and corporately—that could approximate what she was doing here? Explain.

FOR DEEPER STUDY

Many of the old hymns of the church are expressions of worship from the forgiven heart of a wretched sinner. "Amazing Grace" is a case in point, but there are many others. Here are a few for reflection and discussion.

AND CAN IT BE THAT I SHOULD GAIN?

And can it be that I should gain
An interest in the Savior's blood?
Died He for me, who caused His pain—
For me, who Him to death pursued?
Amazing love! How can it be,
That Thou, my God, shouldst die for me?

ALAS! AND DID MY SAVIOR BLEED?

Alas! and did my Savior bleed and did my Sovereign die?
Would He devote that Sacred Head for such a worm as I?

GRACE GREATER THAN OUR SIN

Marvelous grace of our loving Lord,
Grace that exceeds our sin and our guilt!
Yonder on Calvary's mount outpoured,
There where the blood of the Lamb was spilt;
Grace, grace, God's grace,
Grace that will pardon and cleanse within.
Grace, grace, God's grace,
Grace that is greater than all my sin.

Why do you suppose there are so many hymns like this when
so few contemporary worship songs deal as blatantly with sin
and confession?

Read 1 John 1:5 – 7. What does walking in the light mean?

For some reason the popular belief is that walking in the light
means being perfect for a while. But notice especially verse 7: "But
if we walk in the light, as he is in the light, we have fellowship with
one another, and the blood of Jesus, his Son, purifies us from all
sin." The verbs here are all in the continuous tense, better read, "If
we keep walking in the light, we will be having fellowship with one
another, and the blood of Jesus will keep on cleansing us from sin."
If all these things are happening together, then walking in the light
must include sin, since we are going to be cleansed of it as we walk.
Therefore walking in the light doesn't mean some state of perfection
attainable in this life. It means something else.

What could it be? What does light do?

So walking in the light is living in a state of being continually revealed. Because we aren't doing anything in the darkness, even our sin is exposed. And then, most importantly, notice that this all happens in the context of fellowship.

What happens to the other people in a group when someone "walks in the light" and confesses a sin or a failure?

If just one person will step into the light, it will be easier for everyone else to follow suit. Who of you will be the brave one?

DEVELOPING YOUR GIFTS TO SERVE OTHERS   15 MIN.

7. If your group still needs to make decisions about continuing to meet for another study, have that discussion now. Review the Small Group Agreement and discuss any adjustments you would like to make before you begin a new study. Decide what you will study next.

SURRENDERING YOUR LIFE FOR GOD'S PLEASURE   20–25 MIN.

The sinful woman who came to Jesus while he dined at the Pharisee's house kissed his feet and anointed them with perfume, a sign of the utmost respect, submission, and affection.

8. Part of our worship has to do with revering God for who he is. Another part of our worship has to do with our astonishment and gratitude over being forgiven. Robert Capon has defined the church as "a community of astonished hearts, claiming the end of religion in Jesus." Take some time to declare to one another your amazement over your forgiveness. In other words, from what have you been forgiven?

9. Communion, or the Lord's Supper, is something we Christians do to remember and honor what Jesus did for us through his death on the cross. If you have decided to share Communion together today, do so now. You will find instructions for serving Communion on pages 106–107 of the appendix.

10. Spend a few minutes in prayer, asking God to show you an area of your life you need to surrender fully to him. It may

be that you need to allow him to come into your life as your Savior. Maybe you are vulnerable to a particular temptation and you need the Spirit's power to resist. Maybe you need his wisdom to deal with a difficult relationship. If you are willing to make such a commitment, share your decision with the group now or with your host after the meeting.

11. Use the Reflections verses at the end of this session in your quiet time this week. Record any thoughts or direction you receive from the Lord in the space provided.

STUDY NOTES

Alabaster jar of perfume. In Mark's account of this event, the gospel writer refers to this perfume as "an alabaster jar of very expensive perfume.... Some of those present were saying indignantly to one another, 'Why this waste of perfume? It could have been sold for more than a year's wages and the money given to the poor'" (Mark 14:3–5). In the original Greek, the term for "a year's wages" is actually "more than 300 denarii." The denarii was typically a day's pay for a soldier or a common laborer. Three hundred denarii, then, would denote 300 days or a year's worth of work.

Five hundred denarii and the other fifty. According to the definition above, 500 denarii would be the equivalent of 500 days' wages for a common laborer, while fifty denarri would be the equivalent of fifty days' wages. The comparison is the forgiveness of a debt amounting to almost two months' wages versus a debt approaching two years' wages.

Put oil on my head. The host would not have been expected to do this, but the gesture goes beyond mere politeness. This act is mentioned by the psalmist in Psalms 133:2 and 23:5.

PRAYER AND PRAISE REPORT

Briefly share your prayer requests with the large group, making notations below. Then gather in small groups of two to four to pray for each other.

Date: _____

PRAYER REQUESTS

_____
_____
_____
_____
_____
_____
_____
_____
_____
_____
_____
_____

PRAISE REPORT

_____
_____
_____
_____
_____
_____
_____
_____
_____

REFLECTIONS

Each day read the daily verse(s) and give prayerful consideration to what you learn about God, his Spirit, and his place in your life. Then record your thoughts, insights, or prayer in the Reflect section. On day six record a summary of what you have learned over the entire week through this study.

DAY 1   *"Sing to the LORD! Give praise to the LORD! He rescues the life of the needy from the hands of the wicked." (Jeremiah 20:13)*

REFLECT: _____

_____

_____

_____

_____

_____

_____

_____

_____

_____

DAY 2   *"Through Jesus, therefore, let us continually offer to God a sacrifice of praise — the fruit of lips that confess his name." (Hebrews 13:15)*

REFLECT: _____

_____

_____

_____

_____

_____

_____

_____

DAY 3   *"Praise be to the Lord, the God of Israel, because he has come and has redeemed his people." (Luke 1:68)*

REFLECT: _____

_____

_____

_____

_____

_____

_____

_____

_____

_____

_____

DAY 4   *"Love the LORD your God with all your heart and with all your soul and with all your strength." (Deuteronomy 6:5)*

REFLECT: _____

_____

_____

_____

_____

_____

_____

_____

_____

_____

DAY 5   *"Yet a time is coming and has now come when the true worshipers will worship the Father in spirit and truth, for they are the kind of worshipers the Father seeks. God is spirit, and his worshipers must worship in spirit and in truth." (John 4:23 – 24)*

REFLECT: _____

_____

_____

_____

_____

_____

_____

_____

_____

_____

_____

_____

DAY 6   Use the following space to write any thoughts God has put in your heart and mind about the things discussed during session six and/or during your Reflections time this week.

REFLECT: _____

_____

_____

_____

_____

_____

_____

_____

_____

_____

_____

APPENDIX

APPENDIX

FREQUENTLY
ASKED QUESTIONS

WHAT DO WE DO ON THE FIRST NIGHT OF OUR GROUP?

Like all fun things in life—have a party! A "get to know you" coffee, dinner, or dessert is a great way to launch a new study. You may want to review the Small Group Agreement (pages 97–98) and share the names of a few friends you can invite to join you. But most importantly, have fun before your study time begins.

WHERE DO WE FIND NEW MEMBERS FOR OUR GROUP?

This can be troubling, especially for new groups that have only a few people or for existing groups that lose a few people along the way. We encourage you to pray with your group and then brainstorm a list of people from work, church, your neighborhood, your children's school, family, the gym, and so forth. Then have each group member invite several of the people on his or her list. Another good strategy is to ask church leaders to make an announcement or allow a bulletin insert.

No matter how you find members, it's vital that you stay on the lookout for new people to join your group. All groups tend to go through healthy attrition—the result of moves, releasing new leaders, ministry opportunities, and so forth—and if the group gets too small, it could be at risk of shutting down. If you and your group stay open, you'll be amazed at the people God sends your way. The next person just might become a friend for life. You never know!

HOW LONG WILL THIS GROUP MEET?

It's totally up to the group—once you come to the end of this six-week study. Most groups meet weekly for at least their first six weeks, but every other week can work as well. We strongly recommend that the group meet for the first six months on a weekly basis if at all possible. This allows for continuity, and if people miss a meeting they aren't gone for a whole month.

At the end of this study, each group member may decide if he or she wants to continue on for another six-week study. Some groups launch relationships for years to come, and others are stepping-stones into another group experience. Either way, enjoy the journey.

CAN WE DO THIS STUDY ON OUR OWN?

Absolutely! This may sound crazy but one of the best ways to do this study is not with a full house but with a few friends. You may choose to gather with one other couple who would enjoy going to the movies or having a quiet dinner and then walking through this study. Jesus will be with you even if there are only two of you (Matthew 18:20).

WHAT IF THIS GROUP IS NOT WORKING FOR US?

You're not alone! This could be the result of a personality conflict, life stage difference, geographical distance, level of spiritual maturity, or any number of things. Relax. Pray for God's direction, and at the end of this six-week study, decide whether to continue with this group or find another. You don't buy the first car you look at or marry the first person you date, and the same goes with a group. Don't bail out before the six weeks are up—God might have something to teach you. Also, don't run from conflict or prejudge people before you have given them a chance. God is still working in you too!

WHO IS THE LEADER?

Most groups have an official leader. But ideally, the group will mature and members will rotate the leadership of meetings. We have discovered that healthy groups rotate hosts/leaders and homes on a regular basis. This model ensures that all members grow, give their unique contribution, and develop their gifts. This study guide and the Holy Spirit can keep things on track even when you rotate leaders. Christ has promised to be in your midst as you gather. Ultimately, God is your leader each step of the way.

HOW DO WE HANDLE THE CHILD-CARE NEEDS IN OUR GROUP?

Very carefully. Seriously, this can be a sensitive issue. We suggest that you empower the group to openly brainstorm solutions. You may try one option that works for a while and then adjust over time. Our favorite approach is for adults to meet in the living room or dining room, and to share the cost of a babysitter (or two) who can be with the kids in a different part of the house. In this way, parents don't have to be away from their children all evening when their children are too young to be left at home. A second option is to use one home for the kids and a second home (close by or a phone call away) for the adults. A third idea is to rotate the responsibility of providing a lesson or care for the children either in the same home or in another home nearby. This can be an incredible blessing for kids. Finally, the most common idea is to decide that you need to have a night to invest in your spiritual lives individually or as a couple, and to make your own arrangements for child care. No matter what decision the group makes, the best approach is to dialogue openly about both the problem and the solution.

SMALL GROUP AGREEMENT

OUR PURPOSE

To transform our spiritual lives by cultivating our spiritual health in a healthy small group community. In addition, we: _____

_____

_____

_____

OUR VALUES

Group Attendance	To give priority to the group meeting. We will call or email if we will be late or absent. (Completing the Small Group Calendar on page 99 will minimize this issue.)
Safe Environment	To help create a safe place where people can be heard and feel loved. (Please, no quick answers, snap judgments, or simple fixes.)
Respect Differences	To be gentle and gracious to people with different spiritual maturity, personal opinions, temperaments, or imperfections. We are all works in progress.
Confidentiality	To keep anything that is shared strictly confidential and within the group, and to avoid sharing improper information about those outside the group.
Encouragement for Growth	To be not just takers but givers of life. We want to spiritually multiply our life by serving others with our God-given gifts.

Welcome for Newcomers	To keep an open chair and share Jesus' dream of finding a shepherd for every sheep.
Shared Ownership	To remember that every member is a minister and to ensure that each attender will share a small team role or responsibility over time.
Rotating Hosts/Leaders and Homes	To encourage different people to host the group in their homes, and to rotate the responsibility of facilitating each meeting. (See the Small Group Calendar on page 99.)

OUR EXPECTATIONS

- Refreshments/mealtimes _____
- Child care _____
- When we will meet (day of week) _____
- Where we will meet (place) _____
- We will begin at (time) _____ and end at _____
- We will do our best to have some or all of us attend a worship service together. Our primary worship service time will be _____
- Date of this agreement _____
- Date we will review this agreement again _____
- Who (other than the leader) will review this agreement at the end of this study _____

SMALL GROUP CALENDAR

Planning and calendaring can help ensure the greatest participation at every meeting. At the end of each meeting, review this calendar. Be sure to include a regular rotation of host homes and leaders, and don't forget birthdays, socials, church events, holidays, and mission/ministry projects.

Date	Lesson	Host Home	Dessert/Meal	Leader
Monday, January 15	1	Steve/Laura's	Joe	Bill

PERSONAL HEALTH PLAN

This worksheet could become your single most important feature in this study. On it you can record your personal priorities before the Father. It will help you live a healthy spiritual life, balancing all five of God's purposes.

PURPOSE	PLAN
CONNECT	WHO are you connecting with spiritually?
GROW	WHAT is your next step for growth?
DEVELOP	WHERE are you serving?
SHARE	WHEN are you shepherding another in Christ?
SURRENDER	HOW are you surrendering your heart?

DATE	MY PROGRESS	PARTNER'S PROGRESS

SAMPLE
PERSONAL HEALTH PLAN

This worksheet could become your single most important feature in this study. On it you can record your personal priorities before the Father. It will help you live a healthy spiritual life, balancing all five of God's purposes.

PURPOSE	PLAN
CONNECT	WHO are you connecting with spiritually? *Bill and I will meet weekly by email or phone*
GROW	WHAT is your next step for growth? *Regular devotions or journaling my prayers 2x/week*
DEVELOP	WHERE are you serving? *Serving in Children's Ministry Go through GIFTS Class*
SHARE	WHEN are you shepherding another in Christ? *Shepherding Bill at lunch or hosting a starter group in the fall*
SURRENDER	HOW are you surrendering your heart? *Help with our teenager New job situation*

DATE	MY PROGRESS	PARTNER'S PROGRESS
3/5	Talked during our group	Figured out our goals together
3/12	Missed our time together	Missed our time together
3/26	Met for coffee and review of my goals	Met for coffee
4/10	Emailed prayer requests	Bill sent me his prayer requests
3/5	Great start on personal journaling	Read Mark 1 – 6 in one sitting!
3/12	Traveled and not doing well this week	Journaled about Christ as Healer
3/26	Back on track	Busy and distracted; asked for prayer
3/1	Need to call Children's Pastor	
3/26	Group did a serving project together	Agreed to lead group worship
3/30	Regularly rotating leadership	Led group worship — great job!
3/5	Called Jim to see if he's open to joining our group	Wanted to invite somebody, but didn't
3/12	Preparing to start a group in fall	
3/30	Group prayed for me	Told friend something he's learning about Christ
3/5	Overwhelmed but encouraged	Scared to lead worship
3/15	Felt heard and more settled	Issue with wife
3/30	Read book on teens	Glad he took on his fear

PERSONAL HEALTH ASSESSMENT

CONNECTING WITH GOD AND OTHERS

I am deepening my understanding of and friendship with God in community with others.	1 2 3 4 5
I am growing in my ability both to share and to show my love to others.	1 2 3 4 5
I am willing to share my real needs for prayer and support from others.	1 2 3 4 5
I am resolving conflict constructively and am willing to forgive others.	1 2 3 4 5

CONNECTING TOTAL _____

GROWING IN YOUR SPIRITUAL JOURNEY

I have a growing relationship with God through regular time in the Bible and in prayer (spiritual habits).	1 2 3 4 5
I am experiencing more of the characteristics of Jesus Christ (love, patience, gentleness, courage, self-control, and so forth) in my life.	1 2 3 4 5
I am avoiding addictive behaviors (food, television, busyness, and the like) to meet my needs.	1 2 3 4 5
I am spending time with a Christian friend (spiritual partner) who celebrates and challenges my spiritual growth.	1 2 3 4 5

GROWING TOTAL _____

SERVING WITH YOUR GOD-GIVEN DESIGN

I have discovered and am further developing my unique God-given design.	1 2 3 4 5
I am regularly praying for God to show me opportunities to serve him and others.	1 2 3 4 5
I am serving in a regular (once a month or more) ministry in the church or community.	1 2 3 4 5
I am a team player in my small group by sharing some group role or responsibility.	1 2 3 4 5

SERVING TOTAL _____

SHARING GOD'S LOVE IN EVERYDAY LIFE

I am cultivating relationships with non-Christians and praying for God to give me natural opportunities to share his love.	1	2	3	4	5
I am praying and learning about where God can use me and my group cross-culturally for missions.	1	2	3	4	5
I am investing my time in another person or group who needs to know Christ.	1	2	3	4	5
I am regularly inviting unchurched or unconnected friends to my church or small group.	1	2	3	4	5

SHARING TOTAL _____

SURRENDERING YOUR LIFE TO GOD

I am experiencing more of the presence and power of God in my everyday life.	1	2	3	4	5
I am faithfully attending services and my small group to worship God.	1	2	3	4	5
I am seeking to please God by surrendering every area of my life (health, decisions, finances, relationships, future, and the like) to him.	1	2	3	4	5
I am accepting the things I cannot change and becoming increasingly grateful for the life I've been given.	1	2	3	4	5

SURRENDERING TOTAL _____

Connecting · Growing · Developing · Sharing · Surrendering

20 — Well Developed
16 — Very Good
12 — Getting Good
8 — Fair
4 — Just Beginning

○ Beginning Assessment Total _____   □ Ending Assessment Total _____

SERVING COMMUNION

The Lord Jesus, on the night he was betrayed, took bread, and when he had given thanks, he broke it and said, "This is my body, which is for you; do this in remembrance of me." In the same way, after supper he took the cup, saying, "This cup is the new covenant in my blood; do this, whenever you drink, in remembrance of me." For whenever you eat this bread and drink this cup, you proclaim the Lord's death until he comes. (1 Corinthians 11:23 – 26)

SEVERAL PRACTICAL TIPS IN SERVING COMMUNION

1. Be sensitive to timing in your meeting.
2. Break up pieces of cracker or soft bread on a small plate or tray. *Don't* use large servings of bread or grape juice. We ask that you only use grape juice, not wine, so you will not cause a group member to struggle.
3. Prepare all of the elements beforehand and bring these into the room when you are ready.

STEPS IN SERVING COMMUNION

1. Open by sharing about God's love, forgiveness, grace, mercy, commitment, tenderheartedness, or faithfulness, out of your own personal journey (connect with the stories of those in the room).
2. Read the passage: "The Lord Jesus, on the night he was betrayed, took bread, and when he had given thanks, he broke it and said, 'This is my body, which is for you; do this in remembrance of me.'"
3. Pray and pass the bread around the circle (could be time for quiet reflection, singing a simple praise song, or listening to a worship CD).
4. When everyone has been served, remind them that this represents Jesus' broken body on their behalf. Simply state, "Jesus said, 'Do this in remembrance of me.' Let us eat together," and eat the bread as a group.

5. Then read the rest of the passage: "In the same way, after supper he took the cup, saying, 'This cup is the new covenant in my blood; do this, whenever you drink it, in remembrance of me.'"
6. Pray and serve the cups, either by passing a small tray, serving them individually, or having members pick up a cup from the table.
7. When everyone has been served, remind them the juice represents Christ's blood shed for them, then simply state, "Take and drink in remembrance of him. Let us drink together."
8. Finish by singing a simple song, listening to a praise song, or having a time of prayer in thanks to God.

Communion passages: Matthew 26:26–29; Mark 14:22–25; Luke 22:14–20; 1 Corinthians 10:16–21; 11:17–34

LEADING FOR THE FIRST TIME

- **Sweaty palms are a healthy sign.** The Bible says God is gracious to the humble. Remember who is in control; the time to worry is when you're not worried. Those who are soft in heart (and sweaty palmed) are those whom God is sure to speak through.
- **Seek support.** Ask your leader, coleader, or close friend to pray for you and prepare with you before the session. Walking through the study will help you anticipate potentially difficult questions and discussion topics.
- **Bring your uniqueness to the study.** Lean into who you are and how God wants you to uniquely lead the study.
- **Prepare. Prepare. Prepare.** Read the Introduction and Leader's Notes for the session you are leading. Consider writing in a journal or fasting for a day to prepare yourself for what God wants to do.
- **Don't wait until the last minute to prepare.**
- **Ask for feedback so you can grow.** Perhaps in an email or on cards handed out at the study, have everyone write down three things you did well and one thing you could improve on. Don't get defensive, but show an openness to learn and grow.
- **Prayerfully consider launching a new group.** This doesn't need to happen overnight, but God's heart is for this to happen over time. Not all Christians are called to be leaders or teachers, but we are all called to be "shepherds" of a few someday.
- **Share with your group what God is doing in your heart.** God is searching for those whose hearts are fully his. Share your trials and victories. We promise that people will relate.

INTRODUCTION

Congratulations! You have responded to the call to help shepherd Jesus' flock. There are few other tasks in the family of God that surpass the contribution you will be making. As you prepare to lead this small group, there are a few thoughts to keep in mind:

Review the "Read Me First" on pages 9–11 so you'll understand the purpose of each section in the study. If this is your first time leading a small group, turn to Leading for the First Time section on page 108 of the appendix for suggestions.

Remember that you are not alone. God knows everything about you, and he knew that you would be leading this group. God promises, "Never will I leave you; never will I forsake you" (Hebrews 13:5b).

Your role as leader. Create a safe warm environment for your group. As a leader, your most important job is to create an atmosphere where people are willing to talk honestly about what the topics discussed in this study have to do with them. Be available before people arrive so you can greet them at the door. People are naturally nervous at a new group, so a hug or handshake can help put them at ease.

Prepare for each meeting ahead of time. Review the Leader's Notes and write down your responses to each study question. Pay special attention to exercises that ask group members to do something other than engage in discussion. These exercises will help your group live what the Bible teaches, not just talk about it. Be sure you understand how an exercise works, and bring any necessary supplies (such a paper or pens) to your meeting.

Pray for your group members by name. Before you begin each session, go around the room in your mind and pray for each member by name. You may want to review the prayer list at least once a week. Ask God to use your time together to touch the heart of every person uniquely. Expect God to lead you to those he wants you to encourage or challenge in a special way.

Discuss expectations. Ask everyone to tell what he or she hopes to get out of this study. You might want to review the Small Group Agreement (see pages 97–98) and talk about each person's expectations and priorities.

You could discuss whether you want to do the For Deeper Study for homework before each meeting. Review the Small Group Calendar on page 99 and talk about who else is willing to open their home to host or facilitate a meeting.

Don't try to go it alone. Pray for God to help you, and enlist help from the members of your group. You will find your experience to be richer and more rewarding if you enable group members to help — and you'll be able to help group members discover their individual gifts for serving or even leading the group.

Plan a kick-off meeting. We recommend that you plan a kick-off meeting where you will pray, hand out study guides, spend some time getting to know each other, and discuss each person's expectations for the group. A meeting like this is a great way to start a group or step up people's commitments.

A simple meal, potluck, or even good desserts make a kick-off meeting more fun. After dessert, have everyone respond to an icebreaker question, such as, "How did you hear of our church, and what's one thing you love about it?" Or, "Tell us three things about your life growing up that most people here don't know."

If you aren't able to hold a "get to know you" meeting before you launch into session one, consider starting the first meeting half an hour early to give people time to socialize without shortchanging your time in the study. For example, you can have social time from 7:00 to 7:30, and by 7:40 you'll gather the group with a prayer. Even if only a few people are seated in the living room by 7:40, ask them to join you in praying for those who are coming and for God to be present among you as you meet. Others will notice you praying and will come and sit down. You may want to softly play music from a LIFE TOGETHER Worship CD or other worship CD as people arrive and then turn up the volume when you are ready to begin. This first night will set the tone for the whole six weeks.

You may ask a few people to come early to help set up, pray, and introduce newcomers to others. Even if everyone is new, they don't know that yet and may be shy when they arrive. You might give people roles like setting up name tags or handing out drinks. This could be a great way to spot a coleader.

Subgrouping. If your group has more than seven people, break into discussion groups of two to four people for the Growing and Surrendering sections each week. People will connect more with the study and each other when they have more opportunity to participate. Smaller discussion circles encourage quieter people to talk more and tend to minimize the effects of more vocal or dominant members. Also, people who are unaccustomed to praying aloud will feel more comfortable praying within a smaller group of people. Consider sharing prayer requests in the larger group and then break into smaller groups to pray for each other. People are more willing to pray in small circles if they know that the whole group will hear all the prayer requests.

Memorizing Scripture. Although we have not provided specific verses for the group to memorize, this is something you can encourage the group to do each week. One benefit of memorizing God's Word is noted by the psalmist in Psalm 119:11: "I have hidden your word in my heart that I might not sin against you."

Anyone who has memorized Scripture can confirm the amazing spiritual benefits that result from this practice. Don't miss out on the opportunity to encourage your group to grow in the knowledge of God's Word through Scripture memorization.

Reflections. We've provided opportunity for a personal time with God using the Reflections at the end of each session. Don't press seekers to do this, but just remind the group that every believer should have a plan for personal time with God.

Invite new people. Finally, cast the vision, as Jesus did, to be inclusive not exclusive. Ask everyone to prayerfully think of people who would enjoy or benefit from a group like this. The beginning of a new study is a great time to welcome a few people into your circle. Have each person share a name or two and either make phone calls the coming week or handwrite invitations or postcards that very night. This will make it fun and also make it happen. Don't worry about ending up with too many people — you can always have one discussion circle in the living room and another in the dining room.

SESSION 1:
JOSEPH AND HIS BROTHERS

As a leader, your most important job is to create an atmosphere where people are willing to talk honestly about what the topics discussed in this study have to do with them. Some of you may have seekers in your group. They don't even know if they want to believe in Jesus, let alone be in your group. Be sensitive to these folks. Talk to them about something other than church, and avoid putting them on the spot with things like prayer.

Especially if your group is new, be available before people arrive so you can greet them at the door. People are naturally nervous at a new group, so a hug or handshake can help put them at ease.

If this is your first time leading a small group, turn to Leading for the First Time on page 108 of the appendix for additional suggestions.

CONNECTING. Question 1. We've designed this study for both new and established groups. New groups need to invest more time in building relationships with each other, while established groups often want to dig deeper into Bible study and application. After opening your meeting in prayer, begin your group time each week with this icebreaker question to get people relaxed and focused on the topic of discussion for this session. You should be the first to answer this question while others are thinking about how to respond. Be sure to give everyone a chance to respond, because it's a chance for the group to get to know each other. It's not necessary to go around the circle in order. Just ask for volunteers to respond.

Introduction to the Series. Take a moment after question 1 to orient the group to one principle that undergirds this series: A healthy small group balances the purposes of the church. Most small groups emphasize Bible study, fellowship, and prayer. But God has called us to reach out to others as well. He wants us to *do* what Jesus teaches, not just *learn* about it. You may spend less time in this series studying the Bible than some group members are used to. That's because you'll spend more time *doing* things the Bible says believers should do.

However, those who like more Bible study can find plenty of it in this series. For Deeper Study provides additional passages you can study on the topic of each session. If your group likes to do deeper Bible study, consider having members answer next week's Growing section questions ahead of time as homework. They can even study next week's For Deeper Study passages for homework too. Then, during the Growing portion of your meeting, you can share the high points of what you've learned.

Question 2. A Small Group Agreement helps you clarify your group's priorities and cast new vision for what the group can be. Members can imagine what your group could be like if they lived these values. So turn to pages 97–98 and choose one or two values that you want to emphasize in this study. We've suggested reviewing the Frequently Asked Questions (pages 94–96) to gain an understanding of how the group should function and answer any questions that may come up.

Also, take some time before you meet the first time to set your meeting schedule and then allow time during the group meeting for everyone to write down the schedule on their Small Group Calendar on page 99.

Question 3. Also take time during this first session to get an up-to-date Group Roster started. You will need this information throughout the course of the study to stay in touch with people regarding meeting postponements, preparations for special activities, or getting volunteers when needed.

GROWING. Each Growing section begins with an opening story and a passage of Scripture. Have someone read the opening story and someone else read the Bible passage aloud. It's a good idea to ask someone ahead of time, because not everyone is comfortable reading aloud in public. When the passage has been read, ask the questions that follow.

It is not necessary that everyone answer every question in the Bible study. In fact, a group can become boring if you simply go around the circle and give answers. Your goal is to create a discussion—which means that perhaps only a few people respond to each question and an engaging dialogue gets going. It's even fine to skip some questions in order to spend more time on questions you believe are most important.

Remember to use the Study Notes as you prepare for each session to add depth and understanding to your study.

Questions 4–9. Select among these questions to the degree you have time. Groups doing deeper Bible study will want to spend more time with these questions. Others may want to choose one or two questions to discuss.

DEVELOPING. Question 10. For those who haven't done a Life Together study before, spiritual partners will be a new idea. This addresses the practice of having an accountability partner, someone who will commit to pray and hold you accountable for spiritual goals and progress. This may be the single most important habit your group members can take away from this study. Encourage everyone to partner with one other person, two at the most. In this session we encourage you to become familiar with and begin to use the Personal Health Plan to challenge and track your spiritual goals and progress as well as your partner's. There is one Personal Health Plan in the appendix of this book so be sure to have a few photocopies on hand at your first meeting for groups of three spiritual partners.

Question 11. Here we talk about rotating host homes and leaders. This practice will help you to spot potential leaders and those who can fill in for you when you are unavailable for some reason. This is an important practice if you are going to help your group develop their gifts and build strong leaders within your group. Use the Small Group Calendar on page 99 to note who will be hosting, leading, and providing snacks.

SURRENDERING. One of the most important aspects of every small group meeting is the prayer support we offer to one another. The Surrendering section gives you the opportunity to share needs and know that the group will be faithful to pray. As the leader you want to be sure to allow time for this important part of small group life.

Never pressure a person to pray aloud. That's a sure way to scare someone away from your group. Instead of praying in a circle (which makes it obvious when someone stays silent), allow open time when anyone can pray who wishes to do so. Have someone write down everyone's prayer requests on the Prayer and Praise Report. If your time is short, consider having people share requests and pray just with their spiritual partners or in smaller circles of three or four.

Question 14. Every believer should have a plan for spending time alone with God. Here is your opportunity to encourage your group to embrace Scripture reading and time with God by using the Reflections throughout the week. Remind them of how regular time with God and his Word will reap the reward of spiritual growth for those willing to give themselves to it. Maybe you or someone else in the group can share a personal story of the impact this important habit has made on you.

At the end of each session we have provided five daily Scripture readings with room to record your thoughts and on day six there is a place to record your summary of the five reflections. These will offer reinforcement of the principles we are learning and develop the habit of time alone with God throughout the week.

SESSION 2:
FRIENDS OF A PARALYTIC

As you begin, have everyone sit back, relax, close their eyes, and listen to one of the songs on a LIFE TOGETHER Worship CD, or any worship CD. You may want to sing the second time through as a group, or simply take a few moments of silence to focus on God and transition from the distractions of your day.

If this is your first time leading a small group, turn to Leading for the First Time on page 108 of the appendix for additional suggestions.

CONNECTING. Question 1. If newcomers have joined the group, take a few minutes to let all members introduce themselves. You could even let each member tell one thing he or she has liked about the group so far, and let the newcomers tell who invited them. The first visit to a new group is scary, so be sure to minimize the inside jokes. Introduce newcomers to some highly relational people when they arrive, and partner them with great spiritual partners to welcome them at their first meeting.

You will get to know each other more quickly if you spend time with an icebreaker question at each session. Use the questions here as a way for bonding within your group.

Question 2. Checking in with your spiritual partners will be an option in all sessions from now on. You'll need to watch the clock and keep these conversations to ten minutes. If partners want more time together (as is ideal), they can connect before, after, or outside meetings. Give them a two-minute notice and hold to it if you ever want to get them back in the circle! If some group members are absent or newcomers have joined you, you may need to connect people with new or temporary partners. In a week or two, you might want to ask the group how their partnerships are going. This will encourage those who are struggling to connect or accomplish their goals.

GROWING. We highly recommend that, as leader, you read the Study Notes ahead of time and draw the group's attention to anything there that will help them understand the Bible passage and relate to how it applies to their lives.

Questions 3–8. Select among these questions to the degree you have time. Groups doing deeper Bible study will want to spend more time with these questions. Others may want to choose one or two questions to discuss.

DEVELOPING. Question 9. Make it a priority to have a social event at the end of this study. Ask for volunteers to head up the event planning. If no one volunteers to plan the social, don't be discouraged. Who do you think are the one or two party people in your group? They are likely to respond well if you ask them right after your meeting to take on this project and if you ask two people to team up. Another surefire approach is to ask the group who would be two people perfect for this task.

Question 10. Encourage group members to encourage each other in their commitment to the group. Each week, ask someone to contact anyone missing from the group meeting. People will really feel loved when your group notices absences and reaches out to those who miss a meeting.

SHARING. Question 11. The Circles of Life represent one of the values of the Small Group Agreement: "Welcome for Newcomers." Some groups fear that newcomers will interrupt the intimacy that members have built over time. However, groups generally gain strength with the infusion of new blood. It's like a river of living water flowing into a stagnant pond.

Some groups remain permanently open, while others open periodically, such as at the beginning and end of a study. Love grows by giving itself away. If your circle becomes too large for easy face-to-face conversations, you can simply form a second discussion circle in another room in your home.

As leader, you should do this exercise yourself in advance and be ready to share the names of the people you're going to invite or connect with. Your modeling is the number-one example that people will follow. Give everyone a few moments to write down names before each person shares. You might pray for a few of these names on the spot and/or later in the session. Encourage people not to be afraid to ask someone. Almost no one is annoyed to be invited to something! Most people are honored to be asked, even if they can't make it. You may want to hand out invitations and fill them out in the group.

SURRENDERING. Question 13. Let the group share their prayer requests and encourage them to use the Prayer and Praise Report to record them. Having the prayer requests written down will prompt you to pray for each other. It will also serve as a reminder to you of God's faithfulness as your group sees the prayers answered. After requests have been recorded, spend some time praying as a group for the requests.

Question 14. We've provided opportunity for a personal time with God throughout the week using the Reflections at the end of each session. Don't press seekers to do this, but every believer should have a plan for personal time with God.

SESSION 3:
GIDEON — "LESS IS MORE"

As you begin, welcome any new people and praise those who brought them. Renew the vision to welcome people for one more week and model this if you can. If your group is rotating leaders and you're leading for the first time, thank you for your faith. This is the kind of faith step that makes God smile. If this is your first time leading a small group, turn to Leading for the First Time on page 108 of the appendix for additional suggestions.

In order to maximize your time together and honor the diversity of personality types in your group, do your best to begin and end your group on time. You may even want to adjust your starting or stopping time. Don't hesitate to open in prayer even before everyone is seated. This isn't disrespectful of those who are still gathering — it respects those who are ready to begin, and the others won't be offended. An opening prayer can be as simple as, "Welcome, Lord! Help us! Now let's start."

If you've had trouble getting through all the Bible study questions each week, consider breaking into smaller circles of four or five people for the Bible study (Growing) portion of your meeting. Everyone will get more "airtime," and the people who tend to dominate the discussion will be balanced out. A circle of four doesn't need an experienced leader, and it's a great way to identify and train a coleader.

CONNECTING. Question 1. If new members have joined you, your top priority is to make them feel welcome.

As you prepare to lead the group through the questions here, consider this: We likely all have stories of both of these scenarios; it's just that the unsuccessful stories are harder to tell. But because we all have them we can comfort each other by being honest. Nothing is worse than going through something painful — even if you brought it on yourself — and thinking that everybody else is just cruising. One thing you will discover, if everyone is willing to be honest in a group, is that no one is exempt from anything: pain, struggle, doubt, confusion, temptation, disappointment, guilt ... no need to go on, though we could. It's this kind of sharing that will create a bond in your group. The more honest the telling, the tighter the bond.

Question 2. Have your members "check in" with their spiritual partner, and assess how they are doing with their Personal Health Plans and the goals they have set for themselves.

GROWING. Questions 3–10. Select among these questions to the degree you have time.

DEVELOPING. Question 12. Take time here to talk about a need that you can meet together as a group. Make this your group's ministry project. Once you identify your ministry project, divide up the responsibilities and determine your plan of action. How will you meet the need? Who will oversee the project? What responsibilities are left that other group members can do?

SHARING. Question 13. Return to the Circles of Life to see if the people needing invitations to join the group have been contacted yet. If not, encourage members to make the call within the next forty-eight hours.

SURRENDERING. Question 14. Remember, never pressure a person to pray aloud. That's a sure way to scare someone away from your group. So instead of praying in a circle (which makes it obvious when someone stays silent), allow open time when anyone can pray who wishes to do so. Have someone write down everyone's prayer requests on the Prayer and Praise Report. If your time is short, consider having people share requests and pray just with their spiritual partners or in smaller circles of two to four.

There are bound to be people in your group who long for healing, whether physical or emotional, and this will come out during prayer request time. Some churches emphasize prayer for healing — if yours does, follow your church's practice in the way you approach this. Other churches prefer to avoid a charismatic flavor in their small groups — if yours has that concern, pray for one another in whatever way seems comfortable. If you're concerned that some members might confuse or try to "fix" others through prayer, pray as a whole group and monitor how people pray. But don't be overly concerned: the very worst that will happen is that someone will pray in a way that distresses someone else, and if that happens you can simply talk to each person privately before your next meeting. As leader, you set the example of how people will pray for each other in your group, and most members will follow your lead.

The Bible is clear that every Christian is meant to be a servant of Christ. We strongly recommend you challenge your members to take whatever step that they sense God is calling them to and that will challenge them. You will need to model here. Don't miss the need people have to grow through sharing responsibilities to host the group.

If this is your first time leading a small group, turn to Leading for the First Time on page 108 of the appendix for additional suggestions.

CONNECTING. Question 1. If new members have joined you, your top priority is to make them feel welcome. Be prepared to answer this question if no one else responds.

Question 2. As you encourage your group members to check in with their spiritual partners this week, you might want to ask the group to share how their partnerships are going. This will encourage those who are struggling to connect or accomplish their goals.

Question 3. In this session we want you to be thinking about this group continuing to meet for another study. Begin thinking about whether your group will continue to meet and what you can study next.

GROWING. Questions 4 – 10. Select among these questions to the degree you have time.

DEVELOPING. Question 11. The secret servant exercise will only take a minute and will really warm up the group. Have the paper and pens ready to go. Make sure every member is covered, especially those who are absent.

Question 12. Have the planners of your group social update the group on how the planning is going. If you need to, ask for additional volunteers to help make this event a reality.

SESSION 5:
JONAH — WHAT *NOT* TO DO

If this is your first time leading a small group, turn to Leading for the First Time on page 108 of the appendix for additional suggestions.

CONNECTING. Question 1. You will get to know each other more quickly if you spend time with this icebreaker question at each session. This is a great opportunity for bonding within your group.

GROWING. Questions 3, 6–7. Select among these questions to the degree you have time.

Question 4. This question asks your group to do some serious self-assessment. Thinking about these things is necessary in order to disarm the many rationalizations we use to justify judgmental feelings and prejudices. Before digging too far into this question, stop and pray for God's attitude to replace our own toward the people for whom we hold these ill feelings. It will take the Holy Spirit to help us get over our hurt, sense of injustice, and desire for revenge. However right we are, we have no business condemning anyone. Jesus said that if we want God to be merciful to us, we must be merciful to everyone else. You can't get pardon for yourself and then turn around and sentence someone else.

Question 5. If we truly get this, we realize that sin is no longer the issue between God and us; Jesus is. We've all sinned. That's a given. The question is: Do you know Jesus? What are some ways we can tell our friends about the grace and mercy of God? (Hint: start with yourself!)

DEVELOPING. Question 8. Don't miss this opportunity to have group members affirm each other using the "hot seat" exercise. This is a great way to include all group members in an affirmation exercise, and it gives everyone the opportunity to share how other members of the group have impacted them.

Question 9. Finalize plans for a social event following the completion of this study. Planning socials in between studies gives you a break, builds relationships in your group, and helps you get to know each other better. Plan what you will do, when you will do it, and where it will be. It does not have to be elaborate; it could be just a potluck or barbecue.

SURRENDERING. Question 12. Consider if Communion is appropriate for your group. If so, you will find instructions for serving Communion on pages 106–107 of the appendix. If not, plan a time of praising God as a group.

SESSION 6:
A SINFUL WOMAN — TRUE WORSHIP

You made it! This is the last session of this study! It's a time to look at where you've been and look forward to what's next for each of you and your group. Your goal for this meeting is to finish strong. It's also a time to think about God's final, ultimate purpose for you: surrendering your whole lives to him in worship, to give him pleasure.

Whether your group is ending or continuing, it's important to celebrate where you have come together. Thank everyone for what they've contributed to the group. You might even give some thought ahead of time to something unique each person has contributed. You can say those things at the beginning of your meeting.

If this is your first time leading a small group, turn to Leading for the First Time on page 108 of the appendix for additional suggestions.

CONNECTING. Question 2. Be sure to have spiritual partners check in with each other at this last meeting. Encourage them to review their Health Plans together to assess where they have grown and where they would still like to grow.

GROWING. Your love for God, and your resulting character as followers of Christ, will run only as deep as you are willing to be honest in this group. Stop short of telling the whole truth about yourselves and your growth will be stunted, jeopardizing the value of the time spent together. As leader, you can model this honesty by sharing your answers to these questions first while setting an example of what is expected from group members. This is a good time to renew your commitment to the group—not only to being faithful to it, but to being ruthlessly honest as well.

DEVELOPING. Question 7. Spend some time in this last meeting preparing your group to move forward. If your group is staying together, hopefully you've chosen your next study; be sure to take the study guides to the meeting. Suggest that the group take another look at your Group Agreement to see if you want to change anything for the next study. Are all the values working for you, or is there some way your group could be improved by changing your expectations or living up to one of these values better than you have been? You can make people feel safe talking about things they want to improve by first asking them what they've liked about the group. Set a positive tone. Then make sure people get to disagree respectfully, that everyone understands that they're speaking in confidence and won't be talked about outside the group, and that the goal of any changes will be the spiritual health of everyone.

SURRENDERING. Question 9. If you have decided to share Communion as a group at this final meeting, be sure to coordinate this ahead of time. Instructions can be found on pages 106–107 of the appendix. Communion will probably take ten minutes if you have everything prepared. It's a tremendously moving experience in a small group.

If you will not be sharing Communion as a group, you might plan a time of praising God together instead. Take turns praying, using phrases like "Thank you, Lord, for . . ." or "Lord, I praise you for . . ." to begin.

SMALL GROUP ROSTER

Name	Address	Phone	Email Address	Team or Role	Church Ministry
Bill Jones	7 Alvalar Street L.F. 92665	766-2255	bjones@aol.com	Socials	children's ministry

(Pass your book around your group at your first meeting to get everyone's name and contact information.)

Name	Address	Phone	Email Address	Team or Role	Church Ministry

Experiencing Christ Together:

Living with Purpose in Community

Brett & Dee Eastman; Todd & Denise Wendorff; Karen Lee-Thorp

Experiencing Christ Together: Living with Purpose in Community is a series of six, six-week study guides that offers small groups a chance to explore Jesus' teaching on the five biblical purposes of the church. By closely examining Christ's life and teaching in the Gospels, the series helps group members walk in the steps of Christ's early followers. Jesus lived every moment following God's purposes for his life, and Experiencing Christ Together helps groups learn how they can do this too. The first book lays the foundation: who Christ is and what he has done for us. Each of the other five books in the series looks at how Jesus trained his followers to live one of the five biblical purposes (fellowship, discipleship, service, evangelism, and worship).

	Softcovers	DVD
Beginning in Christ Together	ISBN: 0-310-24986-4	ISBN: 0-310-26187-2
Connecting in Christ Together	ISBN: 0-310-24981-3	ISBN: 0-310-26189-9
Growing in Christ Together	ISBN: 0-310-24985-6	ISBN: 0-310-26192-9
Serving Like Christ Together	ISBN: 0-310-24984-8	ISBN: 0-310-26194-5
Sharing Christ Together	ISBN: 0-310-24983-X	ISBN: 0-310-26196-1
Surrendering to Christ Together	ISBN: 0-310-24982-1	ISBN: 0-310-26198-8

Pick up a copy today at your favorite bookstore!

Doing Life Together series

Brett & Dee Eastman; Todd & Denise Wendorff;
Karen Lee-Thorp

Based on the five biblical purposes that form the bedrock of Saddleback Church, Doing Life Together will help your group discover what God created you for and how you can turn this dream into an everyday reality. Experience the transformation firsthand as you begin Connecting, Growing, Developing, Sharing, and Surrendering your life together for him.

"Doing Life Together is a groundbreaking study . . . [It's] the first small group curriculum built completely on the purpose-driven paradigm . . . The greatest reason I'm excited about [it] is that I've seen the dramatic changes it produces in the lives of those who study it."

—From the foreword by Rick Warren

Small Group Ministry Consultation

Building a healthy, vibrant, and growing small group ministry is challenging. That's why Brett Eastman and a team of certified coaches are offering small group ministry consultation. Join pastors and church leaders from around the country to discover new ways to launch and lead a healthy Purpose-Driven small group ministry in your church. To find out more information please call 1-800-467-1977.

	Softcover	
Beginning Life Together	ISBN: 0-310-24672-5	ISBN: 0-310-25004-8
Connecting with God's Family	ISBN: 0-310-24673-3	ISBN: 0-310-25005-6
Growing to Be Like Christ	ISBN: 0-310-24674-1	ISBN: 0-310-25006-4
Developing Your SHAPE to Serve Others	ISBN: 0-310-24675-X	ISBN: 0-310-25007-2
Sharing Your Life Mission Every Day	ISBN: 0-310-24676-8	ISBN: 0-310-25008-0
Surrendering Your Life for God's Pleasure	ISBN: 0-310-24677-6	ISBN: 0-310-25009-9
Curriculum Kit	ISBN: 0-310-25002-1	

Life Together Student Edition

Brett Eastman & Doug Fields

The Life Together series is the beginning of a relational journey, from being a member of a group to being a vital part of an unbelievable spiritual community. These books will help you think, talk, dig deep, care, heal, share ... and have the time of your life! Life ... together!

The Life Together Student Edition DVD Curriculum combines DVD teaching from well-known youth Bible teachers, as well as leadership training, with the Life Together Student Edition Small Group Series to give a new way to do small group study and ministry with basic training on how to live healthy and balanced lives-purpose driven lives.

STARTING to Go Where God Wants You to Be-Student Edition   ISBN: 0-310-25333-0

CONNECTING Your Heart to Others'-Student Edition   ISBN: 0-310-25334-9

GROWING to Be Like Jesus-Student Edition   ISBN: 0-310-25335-7

SERVING Others in Love-Student Edition   ISBN: 0-310-25336-5

SHARING Your Story and God's Story-Student Edition   ISBN: 0-310-25337-3

SURRENDERING Your Life to Honor God-Student Edition   ISBN: 0-310-25338-1

Small Group Leader's Guide Volume 1   ISBN: 0-310-25339-x

Small Group Leader's Guide Volume 2   ISBN: 0-310-25340-3

Small Group Leader's Guide Volume 3

Pick up a copy today at your favorite bookstore!